'"But don't we already do this all the time?! Yes, but neither fully nor well". This book can change that. With clear succinct instructions, incorporating available research evidence, and a list of key tasks to complete at the end of each chapter, Stanton and Dunkley increase our collective mindfulness IQ. A text, a reference, and a consult team companion.'

Andre Ivanoff, *PhD, professor and director, Dialectical Behavior Therapy Training Program, Columbia University School of Social Work, New York; president & board chair, Behavioral Tech Institute, Seattle, USA*

'This practitioners' guidebook is a superb resource for boosting efficacy in teaching mindfulness. It richly integrates seminal ideas from CBT leaders and masterfully shows how to facilitate client engagement with an abundance of splendidly composed dialogues and analogies. Its chapters are anchored in strong bibliographies, and it admirably features adaptations for different settings and clinical populations.'

Raymond W. Novaco, *PhD, professor, Department of Psychological Science, University of California, Irvine, USA*

'Stanton and Dunkley have done it again! The first edition of this little book was an absolute gem and this second edition is a further treasure. New and more extensive examples cover all the challenges that a novice mindfulness teacher or leader of mindfulness skills practice may encounter with numerous practical suggestions to overcome difficulties. If you have never read this book, get it now and if you read the first edition, now is a great opportunity to refresh and rejuvenate your teaching with words of wisdom from Stanton and Dunkley.'

Michaela Swales, *PhD, FBPsS, PFHEA, professor, programme director, North Wales Clinical Psychology Programme, Post-Graduate Diploma in DBT, School of Human and Behavioural Sciences, Bangor University, UK*

'This is such an important book. Whilst the benefits of mindfulness are almost self-evident for those who practice it, teaching mindfulness is a different task. It's riddled with challenges like navigating the sea of definitions, finding appropriate practical exercises, answering challenging questions from students, adapting mindfulness to specific populations, and many others. You'll find the answers here.'

Rodrigo Becerra, *PhD, associate professor, Clinical psychologist, Director of the Psychology Clinic at the University of Western Australia*

'Stanton and Dunkley's extensive experience in teaching mindfulness skills is clear in this practical guide. Filled with clinical examples, analogies, and metaphors readers will find strategies to increase willingness, manage challenges and effectively teach mindfulness. The updated second edition continues to be on my highly recommended list and is a must read for clinicians teaching mindfulness.'

Sian Jeffery, *PhD, senior clinical psychologist & DBT coordinator, Fremantle Mental Health Service; Western Australia, DBT trainer and supervisor, psychology training*

Teaching Clients to Use Mindfulness Skills

This book instructs readers on how to teach mindfulness skills that can be incorporated into everyday life, addressing the specific challenges of effectively passing these skills on to clients in a user-friendly way.

Designed to help professionals introduce mindfulness to clients, the skills laid out in this book can help those struggling with problems of recurrent stress or ruminative thought, and benefit people wanting to live in a more effective, rewarding way. Incorporating a series of practical exercises and drawing on their own professional experience, the authors clearly demonstrate the most effective methods for presenting mindfulness techniques to those with no previous experience. Topics covered include orienting the client to the skill, obtaining and using client feedback effectively, and introducing simple practices. This newly updated edition features up-to-date references and new clinical examples with a new chapter focused on adapting the material for specific clinical populations and for working online.

This practical, structured guide is essential for professionals already teaching or planning to teach mindfulness skills, those taking courses or workshops, and anyone interested in learning more about mindfulness.

Maggie Stanton, DClinPsych, is a consultant clinical psychologist. For many years she led a team of psychological therapists in a large NHS trust. She has supervised and lectured at the University of Southampton and, as a director of Stanton Psychological Services, travels nationally and internationally presenting on mindfulness and other topics.

Christine Dunkley, DClinP, is the director of Applied Research and Training for British Isles DBT, an international expert on DBT and emotion regulation, and the clinical director of Grayrock. She has 35 years of experience in the NHS as a medical social worker and psychological therapist.

Teaching Clients to Use Mindfulness Skills

A Practical Guide

Second Edition

Maggie Stanton and Christine Dunkley

Routledge
Taylor & Francis Group

LONDON AND NEW YORK

Designed cover image: © Getty Images

Second edition published 2025
by Routledge
4 Park Square, Milton Park, Abingdon, Oxon OX14 4RN

and by Routledge
605 Third Avenue, New York, NY 10158

Routledge is an imprint of the Taylor & Francis Group, an informa
business

© 2025 Maggie Stanton and Christine Dunkley

First edition published by Routledge 2014

British Library Cataloguing-in-Publication Data
A catalogue record for this book is available from the British
Library

ISBN: 9781032478159 (hbk)
ISBN: 9781032472195 (pbk)
ISBN: 9781003386117 (ebk)

DOI: 10.4324/9781003386117

Typeset in Optima
by Deanta Global Publishing Services, Chennai, India

For Neville, Josh and Jemima
Maggie

For John, Laura,
Lucy, Matt,
Silver, Acer and Atlas
Christine

Contents

About the authors

Dr Maggie Stanton is a consultant clinical psychologist. She started her career in the nursing profession at St Bartholomew's Hospital, London. She became increasingly interested in the psychological consequences of physical problems and studied psychology at degree level before undertaking her postgraduate training in Clinical Psychology at the University of Birmingham and Doctorate in Clinical Psychology at the University of Surrey. In nearly 30 years of mental health clinical work, she has specialised in seeing clients with severe and enduring mental health problems and has supervised a range of staff in the psychological aspects of their work.

In 1994 Maggie moved to Hampshire. As a Consultant Clinical Psychologist and Psychological Therapies Lead for many years, Maggie headed a team of psychologists and psychological therapists in a large NHS Foundation Trust. Her interest in mindfulness began in 2002 when she undertook core training in Dialectical Behaviour Therapy (DBT, a mindfulness-based cognitive therapy) and progressed to advanced training and supervision in the approach. She took a lead in DBT in her trust and was a Senior Trainer with the national DBT training team. She developed her mindfulness practice including teaching clients in both individual and group settings (including DBT groups), as well as providing supervision, training and support to professionals within her trust and in the wider health care system. She has lectured and supervised at postgraduate level including on the DClinPsych course at the University of Birmingham and the DClinPsych and Postgraduate Diploma CBT at the University of Southampton. She is a consultant and trainer in the public and private sectors in the specialist domain of Clinical Psychology and related fields. She has been involved in a range of research including being clinical lead in a multi-centred randomised control trial for treatment-resistant depression. She has published her work in journals, books and at conferences and has been an invited speaker both nationally and internationally. Maggie was a Director of the UK and Ireland Society for DBT and was a member of the Expert Reference Group, which developed the Self-Harm & Suicide Prevention Competence Framework for the NCCMH. She is an Accredited Therapist and Supervisor with the Society for DBT, registered with the Health Professions Council, a chartered psychologist with the British Psychological Society and a member of the Division of Clinical Psychology.

Dr Christine Dunkley began her career in 1982 as a medical social worker specialising in trauma. Her interest in self-inflicted injury brought her into contact with many clients with borderline personality disorder. Because of the prevalence of childhood sexual abuse in this client group she undertook additional training in counselling and subsequently in DBT. She worked in a psychology department in the NHS and did a doctorate in clinical practice at the University of Southampton. She retired in 2012 to concentrate on supervising and lecturing, and is now Director of Applied Research and Training at British Isles DBT. She has written over 20 publications including 'Regulating Emotion the DBT Way,' and was awarded a Fellowship of the Society for

DBT in 2016. She is also a Clinical Director of Grayrock. She has taught mental health clinicians in America, New Zealand, Poland, Lithuania, Jordan, Israel, Norway and Argentina as well as the UK, and is a popular podcast guest famous for her 'top tips.'

Preface

This book came about because the first edition proved very popular in the UK and internationally, being translated into German and Italian. Many readers provided feedback that they found our experiences and tips invaluable to their work. Whilst some were new to mindfulness, many were experienced practitioners themselves. They asked us if we could add more examples and share our knowledge of teaching in a variety of clinical situations. To this end we have added a new chapter called 'Adapting mindfulness skills for different settings and client populations.' This book is about introducing the concepts of mindfulness to the client, leading them in some mindfulness practices and helping them to go about their day-to-day life in a more mindful way. Our emphasis on how to help clients generalise the skills was particularly valued by practitioners and one on which we have built in this new edition of the book. Like the first edition, it is not a book about teaching formal meditation, nor does it bypass the need for practitioners to develop their own personal mindfulness practice.

We have updated and expanded this practical guide for anyone who might teach mindfulness to their clients including those in business settings, coaches, counsellors, doctors, educators, health and well-being practitioners, HR professionals, managers and leaders, nurses, occupational therapists, psychiatrists, psychologists, psychotherapists, social workers, sports professionals, teachers and those in third sector settings. Throughout the book we have used the terms 'client' and 'therapist' to denote the person being taught mindfulness skills and the person teaching them respectively. We have used these terms for consistency although they may not exactly translate to all the diverse fields in which mindfulness is taught. We have also written a self-help companion guide to this book specifically for clients:

Dunkley, C. and Stanton, M., 2016. *Using Mindfulness Skills in Everyday Life: A Practical Guide*. Taylor & Francis. https://doi .org/10.4324/9781315676326

We have presented the different topics in the order we would introduce them to clients. Some readers will want to start at the beginning of the book and work their way through, others will want to dip into certain chapters to discover more about one particular aspect of teaching mindfulness. Either way, we hope that the key tasks and stylistic factors summarised at the end of each chapter will make this book a valuable resource to keep at hand.

Acknowledgements

We would like to give our heartfelt thanks to all the clients who helped us hone and develop our skills in teaching mindfulness so that we could share these insights with others. Their courage and determination to use mindfulness in their lives have been a constant source of inspiration.

We would also like to thank our colleagues and the delegates who have attended our workshops and webinars. Their feedback, humour and support have been immense and we would not have had the courage to write this book without that. We are grateful to the national and international DBT trainers who have shared their wisdom with us and from whom we have learnt such a lot, particularly Marsha Linehan, Heidi Heard, Michaela Swales, Tom Lynch, Jennifer Sayrs and Sue Clarke. Last, but very far from least, we would like to give a special thank you to Neville and John. Without doubt their advice, encouragement and unstinting faith in us enabled this book to be written.

We use several examples throughout the book of both clients and therapists. These are based on our knowledge and experience over many years but the examples are fictitious and no resemblance to any person is intended.

Abbreviations

ACT	Acceptance and Commitment Therapy
CAMM	Child and Adolescent Mindfulness Measure
DBT	Dialectical Behaviour Therapy
FFMQ	Five Facet Mindfulness Questionnaire
FFMQ-SF	Five Facet Mindfulness Questionnaire – Short Form
MBCT	Mindfulness-Based Cognitive Therapy
MBSR	Mindfulness-Based Stress Reduction
MRI	Magnetic Resonance Imaging
NICE	National Institute for Health and Care Excellence
PBCT	Person-Based Cognitive Therapy

CHAPTER 1

Preparing to teach mindfulness skills

Being a competent teacher of mindfulness skills means being well prepared. This includes being able to answer questions about what mindfulness is, developing our own practice and knowing the evidence base. These are topics we will cover in this chapter.

When we first started teaching mindfulness to clients, "What is mindfulness?" was a question we were often asked. Nowadays people are far more aware of mindfulness, whether from a newspaper report of politicians learning mindfulness or their favourite sports personality talking about how mindfulness helps enhance their performance. This is useful when answering the question, as there are plenty of resources we can suggest to clients that they can easily access to find out more about mindfulness for themselves. Directing clients to sources you feel are likely to be of particular interest to them with a range of formats in which information is presented will cater for clients' different learning styles and preferences. For instance:

- an easy introduction is found in: *Using Mindfulness Sills in Everyday Life: A Practical Guide* (Dunkley and Stanton, 2016) or *The Miracle of Mindfulness* (Hanh, 2008)

DOI: 10.4324/9781003386117-1

- clips on YouTube (e.g., Kabat-Zinn, 2017)
- articles on the internet (e.g., Garey, 2023)
- Facebook groups (e.g., Mindfulness in Daily Life)
- apps (e.g., Headspace, Bemindful).

Over the course of learning mindfulness, clients will develop their own understanding and experience of what mindfulness is for them. To aid this, an effective teacher of mindfulness skills will have at their fingertips some simple definitions of mindfulness. When Jon Kabat-Zinn (1990) described his experience of incorporating mindfulness into a programme for stress reduction he was concerned that preconceptions about eastern meditation could stop people from seeing the relevance of mindfulness to their difficulties. He purposefully used words and phrases that were familiar in western culture to enable patients and medical colleagues to be open to the idea that mindfulness could be relevant to them. In large part this is still true today. The more we can put mindfulness in simple everyday terms that people are familiar with, the more accessible we will make it for our clients.

Definitions of mindfulness

> Mindfulness means paying attention in a particular way: on purpose, in the present moment, and nonjudgmentally.
> (Kabat-Zinn, 1994: 4)

This definition is the one people will come across most frequently and, in our experience, is liked by many clients. Kabat-Zinn also talks about mindfulness being concerned with the present moment: 'Like it or not, this moment is all we really have to work with' (1994: xi). He points out that we often spend our lives thinking about what might happen or what has happened and treating these thoughts as if they are facts. This is mindlessness. Being awake to the present moment and choosing where to put our attention, noticing when we have got caught up in our mind's story of how it is, is mindfulness.

To bring these definitions alive and make them real for people, therapists need a number of examples that will resonate with aspects of their clients' lives. We might use the following:

Amy got an email from her boss saying that he wanted to see her. She began thinking that he would tell her that her job was under threat. She imagined that he was unhappy with the standard or speed of her work. As she walked to his office, with her heart racing and mouth dry, she remembered her mindfulness practice. She recognised that being caught up in why her boss wanted to see her was mindlessness. She brought her focus onto the experience of walking along the corridor, with the carpet under her shoes and the sound of people talking from the offices. When Amy 'woke up' to realise she was paying attention to her mind's version of events, she was being mindful. In noticing her experience of walking along the corridor, she brought her attention into the present moment.

Automatic pilot

An example of being unmindful, or of mindlessness, that people will often find easy to recognise is when we are on 'automatic pilot,' i.e., doing things without being aware of what we are doing.

> I work in two locations during the week: the clinic and the university. The first part of the journey is the same. Sometimes I can set off for the university and, before I realise it, I am turning into the clinic. I have been driving on automatic pilot. If I had been driving mindfully, I would have been aware of where I was, the road in front of me, changing gear, and would have gone to my intended destination.

This story usually brings a smile of recognition from the client. As therapists, we can use a shared experience like this to have a discussion with the client about how much of the time they live in 'automatic pilot' and how it might make a difference to their life to learn to be mindful. It can also provide an opportunity to make the teaching point that these processes are natural things that all minds do.

Taking control of your mind

Marsha Linehan's description of mindfulness emphasises that it is a skill that can be acquired. She makes the point that mindfulness puts you in the driver's seat so that you are in control of your mind, rather than your mind being in control of you (Linehan, 2015a, 2015b). In defining mindfulness, she breaks it down into what we need to do to be mindful (i.e., observe, describe, participate) and how we need to do it (i.e., one thing in the moment, non-judgementally, effectively). This emphasis on mindfulness as a skill is very much what we teach.

Developing our own practice

An important part of our capability to teach mindfulness is the development of our own mindfulness practice. We came to mindfulness through becoming Dialectical Behaviour Therapists, developing our own ability to be mindful and gradually incorporating this mindfulness into our lives. We continue to develop this practice both individually and with others. There are several reasons why this is significant. We will come back to this point throughout the book but we will summarise briefly here.

- Our own practice will enable us to model being mindful when we are with clients.
- Our own practice will give insight into difficulties clients may face (although we are all individuals).
- Our own practice will provide examples we can share with clients (as appropriate) of when we have used mindfulness in our everyday life.
- As mindfulness teachers we should not ask our clients to commit to more mindfulness practice than we are willing to engage in.
- Clients will very quickly catch us out if we are trying to teach a skill we don't have ourselves!

Whilst we previously highlighted the advantages of using everyday language to describe mindfulness, Williams and Kabat-Zinn (2011) point out that by doing so there is a danger of losing the essence of mindfulness practice present in its eastern origins. They emphasise that, as mindfulness teachers, we must have knowledge and experience of mindfulness so that our compassion, acceptance and enquiry are apparent in what we do as much as in what we say. They suggest that any mindfulness-based interventions will only be as effective as the mindfulness instructor teaching them.

'Mindfulness can only be understood from the inside out' (2011: 284). Crane and Kuyken (2019) observed the importance of mindfulness teachers embodying mindfulness when leading practices and taking feedback, suggesting this could be an important mediating factor in the success of mindfulness interventions.

Mindfulness-based therapies

Since Jon Kabat-Zinn incorporated mindfulness into his Mindfulness-Based Stress Reduction (MBSR) programme, several therapies have been developed with mindfulness as a core component. As a teacher of mindfulness skills, it is important to have some knowledge of the common therapies your clients may have heard about. If delivering one of these therapies, therapists should be suitably qualified, supervised and aware of the differences in how mindfulness is taught. For instance, Mindfulness-Based Cognitive Therapy (MBCT) and MBSR both have strict guidelines about the training and supervision required (see the British Association of Mindfulness-Based Approaches Good Practice Guidelines, n.d.).

Marsha Linehan incorporated mindfulness as a core skill in the therapy she developed for highly suicidal and self-harming individuals: Dialectical Behaviour Therapy (DBT) (Linehan, 1993). This therapy is based on the idea that clients need to learn skills in managing distress, regulating their emotions and being effective in relationships. Mindfulness is practised in every DBT skills group session, and there are two sessions dedicated to teaching mindfulness at the start of every eight-week skills training module. It is at the heart of many of the skills taught, e.g., keeping mindful in interpersonal relationships (Interpersonal Effectiveness module) or mindfully observing and describing emotions (Emotion Regulation module).

One therapy that has had increasing attention is Acceptance and Commitment Therapy (ACT), developed by Steve Hayes (Hayes and Smith, 2005). It emphasises getting in touch with the present moment and developing a non-judgemental and accepting approach to our experiences, including difficulties such as anxiety and depression. ACT is recommended by the National Institute for Health and Care Excellence (NICE) to be considered in the treatment of adults with chronic pain and tinnitus. In ACT, as in DBT, mindfulness is described as a skill to be learned and used in everyday life. Like Kabat-Zinn, Hayes recognises that meditation in western culture has been given a 'bad rap' and that how we introduce mindfulness is important in determining whether people will be willing to practise it or not. Similar to DBT, he advocates short practices that can be built upon over time.

As the name suggests, Mindfulness-Based Cognitive Therapy (MBCT) has mindfulness at its core. Since its introduction in 2000 (Teasdale et al.) it has had increasing popularity. Initially it was introduced as a therapy to prevent relapse for people with three or more episodes of depression (Segal et al., 2002). From 2022 it has been recommended by NICE for those clients at risk of relapse and as a group intervention for people with first episode, less severe depression. In more recent times research has been carried out into its use in a number of diverse areas, such as with survivors of breast cancer (Chang et al., 2023).

Unsurprisingly, a common theme in therapies that incorporate mindfulness is the emphasis on changing our relationship to experiences rather than changing the experiences themselves. Paul Chadwick developed Person-Based Cognitive Therapy (PBCT) for distressing psychosis (Chadwick, 2006). In addition to cognitive strategies, clients learn mindfulness skills. In this way they are able to develop a different relationship to a voice-hearing experience so that it no longer evokes the same levels of distress. Rather, the acceptance of the experience without judgement allows the individual to have the experience without reacting to it. In studies by Dannahy et al. (2011) and Chadwick (2019) the researchers describe how they used PBCT in group therapy for people who hear distressing voices. Over the period of the group, clients reported learning to cope with voices differently and started to see the voices as symptoms of a disorder rather than an intrinsic part of themselves. We have experience of running these groups within our own service and have seen how the changes for clients can be truly remarkable, enabling them to start doing activities they had previously given up or going into situations they had been avoiding.

In recent years there has been a growing emphasis on the need for interventions to be sensitive to cultural considerations when teaching mindfulness. For example, Özok and Tanhan (2023) describe a culturally adapted mindfulness stress reduction programme for Turkish, Islamic clients. Also, Castellanos et al. (2020) carried out a systematic review of culturally adapted mindfulness interventions for people from the Hispanic culture. In his paper on 'Mindfulness for global public health,' Oman (2023) emphasises the importance of ensuring interventions not only use culturally appropriate language, sayings, metaphors and stories but also take account of values, customs, relationships and traditions. In addition, he suggests knowledge of the culture should be explicitly included, e.g., when discussing concepts with clients.

Contraindications and Risk

In this book we do not go through risk assessment and management, formulation and treatment planning as these will be part of the normal clinical work we carry out with clients. When considering teaching mindfulness skills, it will always be as part of our clinical formulation and treatment plan for that individual.

As with any therapeutic approach, we will have carried out a risk assessment and developed a risk management plan. As therapists we need to ensure that we have an up-to-date knowledge of the research base including contraindications for the area we are working in, that we have the appropriate level of skill to carry out any intervention we are offering and that we maintain this level of competence through continuing professional development and supervision activities.

Evidence base

Research into mindfulness has grown at a tremendous pace. In their introduction to a special issue of *Contemporary Buddhism*, Williams and Kabat-Zinn (2011) cite the results of a search for the term 'mindfulness' on the ISI Web of Knowledge (now the Web of Science) database on 5 February 2011 by David Black. This showed the number of publications with 'mindfulness' in the abstract or keywords (English language only) had grown from very few in the 1980s and 1990s to 50 by 2003 and over 350 by 2010. A similar search carried out by the authors of this book on the Web of Science from 1 January 2011 to 25 July 2023 revealed 26,281 publications with 2,825 published in the last 12 months alone. Putting the term 'mindfulness' into Google Scholar produces nearly one million returns. The application of mindfulness has grown from medicine and psychology to include education, business, leadership, sports and most aspects of everyday life. When MBSR was introduced to the University of Massachusetts Medical Center by Jon Kabat-Zinn in 1979 he could never have known how widely these ideas and perspectives would take on and the impact they would have on so many different areas of western society. The merging of the two great traditions of empirical science and Buddhist meditative practice has provided a catalyst for the expansion of mindfulness into many domains.

Brain changes

Another way of looking at the impact of mindfulness practice on individuals is to examine the physical effects on the brain using Magnetic Resonance Imaging (MRI) scanning. A study by Siffredi et al. (2023) looked at the brains and functioning of adolescents who had been born very preterm. The adolescents showed gains in white-matter microstructural changes as well as enhancement in global executive functioning after an eight-week mindfulness-based intervention. There have been numerous studies using MRI to investigate the effects of mindfulness on the brain and understand the processes involved. In his review, Weder (2022) noted neuroimaging studies have shown distinct patterns of activation and connectivity in the brain when participants were practicing mindfulness. He linked these to the metacognitive skills of monitoring thoughts and behaviour, which are integral to mindfulness practices. Zhang et al. (2021) also reviewed mindfulness-based interventions and concluded studies consistently found mindful meditation had an effect on brain activity in both healthy and patient populations. In our experience, many clients enjoy seeing pictures from these studies or from news articles about mindfulness.

Research in this area has sparked a lot of media interest. BBC news researcher David Sillito joined an eight-session MBSR group incorporating daily practice of mindfulness (Sillito, 2012). MRI scans of a participant with chronic pain due to Lupus were taken pre and post the group treatment. The scans were taken under two conditions: when the mind was wandering and when meditating. When the person was meditating, the MRI scans showed a decrease in brain activity in those areas associated with pain. This fitted with her experience of the pain being more manageable: 'being taken down a notch' when using mindfulness meditation. Dennis Thompson, HealthDay reporter for US

News (2022) described how Professor Zeidan and his team at the University of California used MRI scans to understand how mindfulness can help people who are in pain. The scans show the communication between areas of the brain that process pain and the neural network related to sense of self are interrupted. After training in mindful meditation, participants reported a 33% reduction in pain when using mindful meditation skills. In contrast, the control group reported a 20% increase in pain. This type of media coverage is often seen by clients who are interested in information about mindfulness that is available on the internet and can spark helpful discussions with their therapist or in group sessions.

Mindfulness measures

We encourage therapists to evaluate their use of mindfulness in therapy to see whether there are changes over time. A number of studies tackle this by measuring symptoms for which the person sought help and whether these have reduced at the end of therapy. This tells us that levels have reduced (or not) but not how that came about. If the hypothesis is that learning mindfulness skills is the mechanism of change, then we need robust measures of mindfulness that should show increases over the period of therapy in line with the reduction of symptoms.

The Five Facet Mindfulness Questionnaire (FFMQ) was developed by Baer et al. (2006). It has been used in many research studies and clinical settings. It is a composite of five questionnaires and has 39 items that relate to different aspects of mindfulness: observing, describing, acting with awareness, taking a non-judgemental approach to inner experience and non-reactivity to inner experience. Encouragingly, Baer et al. (2008) carried out a study which suggested that the more participants practised mindfulness, the more they rated highly on the FFMQ and the more they reported decreased symptoms and increased sense of well-being. There were criticisms that the questionnaire was quite lengthy and difficult to score, so Bohlmeijer et al. (2011) addressed these problems by developing a short form of the questionnaire (FFMQ-SF) with only 24 items and a simplified scoring system.

In 2012 Baer et al. went still further, developing a 15-item version (FFMQ-15). This has been used successfully in a wide range of studies including with people from various countries and cultural backgrounds (e.g., in Spain, Feliu-Soler et al., 2021; in Pakistan, Iqbal et al., 2023; with ethnically diverse students, Kim et al., 2023; and with black Americans, Okafor et al., 2023). Baer was also involved in the development of the Child and Adolescent Mindfulness Measure (CAMM) for school-aged young people (Greco et al., 2011).

Of course, the FFMQ, its short forms and the CAMM are all self-report questionnaires and, as such, are open to biases, e.g., problems of relying on the client's memory and willingness to report accurately, as well as potential differences in how items are interpreted and thus scored. Acknowledging these limitations, self-report questionnaires are widely used and are generally seen as acceptable measures of mindfulness in everyday life (Baer, 2019).

Conclusion

In this chapter we have reviewed areas to consider when preparing to teach mindfulness. We need to be confident in our knowledge of what mindfulness is and our ability to communicate this to others. A key part of this will be our own regular practice of mindfulness and our continued development and support in this area. Given the exponential growth in the database on mindfulness it is beyond the remit of this book to look at the evidence base for all its applications. Nevertheless, it is vital to be aware of the research literature in the particular area of practice and to keep abreast of the fast pace of developments in the field. In Chapter 2 we will look at introducing mindfulness to the client(s).

Key tasks

- Know the evidence base for the application of mindfulness in the area it is being taught, including cultural considerations and exclusion criteria.

- Develop a regular mindfulness practice and model a mindful approach when teaching and taking feedback.

- Develop a network of support/supervision and ongoing professional development.

- Memorise two or three short simple definitions of mindfulness.

- Be aware of how clients may access further information about mindfulness via a variety of formats.

- Investigate a suitable measure of mindfulness appropriate for the setting.

Stylistic factors

- Model warmth, compassion and interest.
- Be open to questions.

Bibliography

Baer, R., 2019. Assessment of mindfulness by self-report. *Current Opinion in Psychology, 28*, pp. 42–48. https://doi.org/10.1016/j.copsyc.2018.10.015

Baer, R.A., Smith, G.T., Hopkins, J., Krietemeyer, J. and Toney, L., 2006. Using self-report assessment methods to explore facets of mindfulness. *Assessment, 13*(1), pp. 27–45. https://doi.org/10.1177/1073191105283504

Baer, R.A., Smith, G.T., Lykins, E., Button, D., Krietemeyer, J., Sauer, S., Walsh, E., Duggan, D. and Williams, J.M., 2008. Construct validity of the five facet mindfulness questionnaire in meditating and nonmeditating samples. *Assessment, 15*(3), pp. 329–342. https://doi.org/10.1177/1073191107313003

Baer, R.A., Carmody, J. and Hunsinger, M., 2012. Weekly change in mindfulness and perceived stress in a mindfulness-based stress reduction program. *Journal of Clinical Psychology, 68*(7), pp. 755–765. https://doi.org/10.1002/jclp. 21865

Bohlmeijer, E., Ten Klooster, P.M., Fledderus, M., Veehof, M. and Baer, R., 2011. Psychometric properties of the five facet mindfulness questionnaire in depressed adults and development of a short form. *Assessment, 18*(3), pp. 308–320. https://doi.org/10.1177/1073191111408231

British Association of Mindfulness-Based Approaches Good Practice Guidelines, n.d. Available at https://bamba.org.uk/good-practice-guidelines/pdf

Castellanos, R., Yildiz Spinel, M., Phan, V., Orengo-Aguayo, R., Humphreys, K.L. and Flory, K., 2020. A systematic review and meta-analysis of cultural adaptations of mindfulness-based interventions for Hispanic populations. *Mindfulness, 11*, pp. 317–332. https://doi.org/10.1007/s12671-019-01210-x

Chadwick, P., 2006. *Person-Based Cognitive Therapy for Distressing Psychosis.* John Wiley & Sons. https://doi.org/10.1002/9780470713075

Chadwick, P., 2019. Mindfulness for psychosis: A humanizing therapeutic process. *Current Opinion in Psychology, 28*, pp. 317–320. https://doi.org/10.1016/j.copsyc.2019.07.022

Chang, Y.C., Tseng, T.A., Lin, G.M., Hu, W.Y., Wang, C.K. and Chang, Y.M., 2023. Immediate impact of Mindfulness-Based Cognitive Therapy (MBCT) among women with breast cancer: A systematic review and meta-analysis. *BMC Women's Health, 23*(1), pp. 1–14. https://doi.org/10.1186/s12905-023-02486-x

Crane, R.S. and Kuyken, W., 2019. The mindfulness-based interventions: Teaching assessment criteria (MBI:TAC): Reflections on implementation and development. *Current Opinion in Psychology, 28*, pp. 6–10. https://doi.org/10.1016/j.copsyc.2018.10.004

Dannahy, L., Hayward, M., Strauss, C., Turton, W., Harding, E. and Chadwick, P., 2011. Group person-based cognitive therapy for distressing voices: Pilot data from nine groups. *Journal of Behavior Therapy and Experimental Psychiatry, 42*(1), pp. 111–116. https://doi .org/10.1016/j.jbtep. 2010.07.006

Dunkley, C. and Stanton, M., 2016. *Using Mindfulness Skills in Everyday Life: A Practical Guide.* Taylor & Francis. https://doi.org/10.4324 /9781315676326

Feliu-Soler, A., Pérez-Aranda, A., Luciano, J.V., Demarzo, M., Marino, M., Soler, J., Van Gordon, W., Garcia-Campayo, J. and Montero-Marin, J., 2021. Psychometric properties of the 15-item five facet mindfulness questionnaire in a large sample of Spanish pilgrims. *Mindfulness, 12*, pp. 852–862. https://doi.org/10.1007/s12671-020-01549-6

Garey, J., 2023. *Mindfulness in the Classroom*, S. Longyear (ed.). Available at: https://childmind.org/article/mindfulness-in-the -classroom/

Greco, L.A., Baer, R.A. and Smith, G.T., 2011. Assessing mindfulness in children and adolescents: Development and validation of the Child and Adolescent Mindfulness Measure (CAMM). *Psychological Assessment, 23*(3), p. 606. https://doi.org/10.1037/a0022819

Hanh, T.N., 2008. *The Miracle of Mindfulness: The Classic Guide to Meditation by the World's Most Revered Master.* Random House.

Hayes, S.C. and Smith, S., 2005. *Get Out of Your Mind and into Your Life: The New Acceptance and Commitment Therapy.* New Harbinger Publications.

Headspace Inc., 2012. *Headspace.* (Version 3) [Mobile app]. Available at: App Store.

Iqbal, F., Iqbal, F. and Humayan, G.K., 2023. Factor structure of the Five Facets Mindfulness Questionnaire (FFMQ) (15 items) in a collectivist society – Pakistan. *Psychology in the Schools, 60*(7), pp. 2502–2519. https://doi.org/10.1002/pits.22875

Kabat-Zinn, J., 1990. *Full Catastrophe Living: How to Cope with Stress, Pain and Illness Using Mindfulness Meditation.* Piatkus Books.

Kabat-Zinn, J., 1994. *Wherever You Go, There You Are: Mindfulness Meditation for Everyday Life.* Piatkus Books.

Kabat-Zinn, J., 2017. *Mindfulness in Everyday Life: Jon Kabat-Zinn with Oprah Winfrey.* 13:12. Available at: www.youtube.com/watch?v =D5r2sBQM31k

Kim, H., Li, N., Broyles, A., Musoka, L. and Correa-Fernández, V., 2023. Validity of the 15-item five-facet mindfulness questionnaire among an ethnically diverse sample of university students, *Journal of American College Health*, 71(2), pp. 450–459. https://doi.org/10.1080/07448481.2021.1892700

Linehan, M., 1993. *Cognitive-Behavioral Treatment of Borderline Personality Disorder*. Guilford Press.

Linehan, M., 2015a. *DBT Skills Training Manual*. Guilford Press.

Linehan, M., 2015b. *DBT Skills Training Handouts and Worksheets*. Guilford Press.

Manning, C., 2020. *Mindfulness in Daily Life*. Available at: www.facebook.com/groups/MINDFULNESSINDAILYLIFE/

National Institute for Health and Care Excellence (NICE), 2020. *Tinnitus: Assessment and Management*. NG155. Available at www.nice.org.uk/guidance/ng155/

National Institute for Health and Care Excellence (NICE), 2021. *Chronic Pain (Primary and Secondary) in Over 16s: Assessment of All Chronic Pain and Management of Chronic Primary Pain*. NG193. Available at: www.nice.org.uk/guidance/NG193/chapter/Recommendations

National Institute for Health and Care Excellence (NICE), 2022. *Depression in Adults: Treatment and Management*. NG222. Available at: www.nice.org.uk/guidance/NG222/chapter/recommendations

Okafor, G.N., Ford, B.Q., Antonoplis, S., Reina, A.M., LutFeali, S. and Shallcross, A.J., 2023. Measuring mindfulness in Black Americans: A psychometric validation of the five facet mindfulness questionnaire. *Mindfulness*, 14(3), pp. 565–581. https://doi.org/10.1007/s12671-023-02072-0

Oman, D., 2023. Mindfulness for global public health: Critical analysis and agenda. *Mindfulness*, pp. 1–40. https://doi.org/10.1007/s12671-023-02089-5

Özok, H.İ. and Tanhan, F., 2023. Developing a culture-adapted mindfulness stress reduction program. *Journal of Progressive Education*, 19(2), pp. 74–91. https://doi.org/10.29329/ijpe.2023.534.5

Segal, Z.V., Williams, J.M.G. and Teasdale, J.D., 2002. *Mindfulness-Based Cognitive Therapy for Depression: A New Approach to Preventative Relapse*. Guilford Press.

Siffredi, V., Liverani, M.C., Van De Ville, D., Freitas, L.G., Borradori Tolsa, C., Hüppi, P.S. and Ha-Vinh Leuchter, R., 2023. The effect of mindfulness-based intervention on neurobehavioural functioning and its association with white-matter microstructural changes in preterm young adolescents. *Scientific Reports*, 13(1), p. 2010. https://doi.org/10.1038/s41598-023-29205-8

Sillito, D., 2012. Mind over matter: Can meditation bring happiness? *BBC News*, 4 January. Available at: www.bbc.co.uk/news/health -16389183

Teasdale, J.D., Segal, Z.V., Williams, J.M.G., Ridgeway, V.A., Soulsby, J.M. and Lau, M.A., 2000. Prevention of relapse/recurrence in major depression by mindfulness-based cognitive therapy. *Journal of Consulting and Clinical Psychology, 68*(4), pp. 615–625. https://doi .org/10.1037/0022-006X.68.4.615

Thompson, D., 2022. Mindfulness can help ease pain, and scientists think they know how. *HealthDay*, 18 July. Available at: https:// consumer.healthday.com/7-18-mindfulness-can-help-ease-pain-and -scientists-think-they-know-how-2657654548.html

Weder, B.J., 2022. Mindfulness in the focus of the neurosciences: The contribution of neuroimaging to the understanding of mindfulness. *Frontiers in Behavioral Neuroscience, 16*, pp. 1–22. https://doi.org/10 .3389/fnbeh.2022.928522

Wellmind Health. 2016. *BeMindful*. [Mobile app]. Available at: App Store.

Williams, J.M.G. and Kabat-Zinn, J., 2011. Mindfulness: Diverse perspectives on its meaning, origins, and multiple applications at the intersection of science and dharma. *Contemporary Buddhism, 12*(1), pp. 1–18. https://doi.org/10.1080/14639947.2011.564811

Zhang, D., Lee, E.K., Mak, E.C., Ho, C.Y. and Wong, S.Y., 2021. Mindfulness-based interventions: An overall review. *British Medical Bulletin, 138*(1), pp. 41–57. https://doi.org/10.1093/bmb/ldab005

Orienting clients to mindfulness

In the previous chapter we outlined the evidence base that gives us confidence to present mindfulness to clients as a useful skill. Given its increasing popularity, more often than not clients have heard of it, and may even have practiced yoga or some other form of meditation in the past. Orienting those clients to mindfulness is easy, and involves simple information-giving. They continue to do well with their practice.

This chapter, though, is not primarily about those people. It might be surprising that there are still people who know nothing about mindfulness, or who have deep reservations about learning this skill. In fact, since we wrote the first edition of this book, we have a new category of challenge to deal with: those who have done a little mindfulness, and are now bored or disillusioned with the idea. 'The raisin practice' has a lot to answer for, with mindfulness and dried fruit now being indelibly fused in the minds of some people.

On our journey as teachers, we have been through the age of ignorance where we had to explain mindfulness as an alien concept, the age of acceptance where people were open to learning, and now the age of satiation, when some clients have heard enough and we have to recapture their interest and

DOI: 10.4324/9781003386117-2

re-explain the benefits. These are the people for whom we need additional skills of orientation.

In this chapter we include our insights and techniques for orienting clients who might initially exhibit some reluctance or scepticism.

Understanding resistance

There are a range of reasons why people have reservations to learning mindfulness. Some dislike anything that is unfamiliar. Others have misconceptions about what mindfulness involves. Occasionally the client is suffering from 'treatment fatigue,' having tried a number of different things that have not helped. If the client has been offered a complex therapy of which mindfulness is one component (such as DBT) they may have reluctantly agreed to participate in order to get the rest of the package. For a significant number of clients, especially those with longstanding depression or personality disorder, their emotional pain can be so great that they are looking for a treatment that 'matches' the level of their distress; it can look to an outsider peering into a mindfulness session as though nothing at all is happening, and the client may wonder how their terrible suffering can be addressed by such an apparent non-event. This can elicit frustration or hostility. The paradox here is that in mindfulness *less is more*, but this is something that is only learned through experience.

These are very understandable reasons for a client to hold back from full engagement. The most effective starting point for the therapist is to validate the difficulty. Offering authentic validation requires the therapist to act mindfully, relinquishing their desire for it to be any other way, accepting in the moment that the client's response is as it is. Specifically, this means not going into a lot of 'why?' questions. Clients often intuit that when a therapist starts asking, "Why do you feel this way?" or "Why do you think that?" it is a prelude to trying to get something changed. This can have the effect of encouraging the client to dig their heels in further. Here is an example of validation without attachment to outcome.

Jamie had suffered a knee injury that had prematurely ended a promising sporting career. He could not engage in meaningful activities without dwelling on how his disability had changed his life. He ruminated constantly on both the physical state of his knee and his past sporting achievements. He would not go out with friends, and talked frequently to his family about his loss. Counselling had helped with the trauma of the injury itself, but not with his rumination and experiential avoidance. When discussing the possibility of attending some sessions to learn mindfulness, Jamie said he could not see how this could help, as his problems were unchangeable – his knee would still be painful and he would not have reached his sporting potential. The therapist agreed that this was indeed a set of problems with no obvious solution. Also, that she could not see how mindfulness could change either of those things. She said that this seemed to be causing Jamie a lot of emotional pain and wondered how this manifested itself. He pointed to his chest and she asked what he did when he noticed this pain. He told her that he began thinking of the cause of it, diverting his attention back to his knee and to his situation. The therapist acknowledged how exhausting this must be. She said that the mindfulness classes were weekly and that she could totally understand the cost to Jamie of attending; the energy involved in getting there, perhaps increasing his physical pain. She observed that this was a big ask with no guarantees that mindfulness would deliver any relief.

At no time does the therapist attempt to sway the client in his thinking. She has unhooked from trying to solve the problem, and has even let go of the idea of encouraging the client to come to mindfulness. She is modelling a mindful approach by accepting things as they are. In doing so, Jamie's initial reluctance reduced and was replaced by curiosity. The therapist waited to give information about the advantages of mindfulness until he invited her to do so, which indicated that he was willing to receive it without blocking. But if he had offered further resistance, she could have validated that in the same way.

Jamie did eventually complete a course of eight sessions, and whilst he continued to experience pain in his knee his rumination decreased enough for him to start attending some social activities. We cannot know what might have happened if the therapist's opening gambit had been to describe how mindfulness might improve things, but it is possible that Jamie could have reacted by trying to prove that his case was indeed hopeless.

The following demonstration can be helpful in winning people over.

The mindfulness teacher waved her hand in the air to get the attention of the class. Before her, on the desk, is a pen.

"Imagine," she said, "That I say to my hand, 'Hand, pick up this pen' But my hand says, 'Don't want to!'

and goes off like this…" (the teacher flicks the pen off the desk, and makes exaggerated wild movements with her hand). "Now, if that happened, I would be off to the doctor PRONTO, and the doctor would probably be extremely interested in such a weird occurrence. Now, I can't believe any of you have ever had that problem, your hand usually obeys your instructions.

But do any of you recognise this other situation: You have had an argument with someone at work. They say some rather unpleasant things to you. You get home that evening, and just want to sit down and watch your favourite TV programme. You sit in your TV-watching chair, turn on the set, select your episode from the list, and press 'play' on the remote control. Your eyes are staring at the screen, so you have all your ducks in a row… then your mind says, 'Why did you let her say that to you at work today? How DARE she say those things? What about the time she did (this) or she said (that)? You know what you SHOULD have done, you should have said…' Tell me, any of you, has your mind ever done that or something similar?"

Most of the students nod. The teacher carries on: "Although we would be horrified if our body did something against our wishes, we regularly accept that our mind does something that, were we in control, we would not have it do. So, mindfulness is the skill of noticing those *uninvited* actions of our mind. The things our mind does that are not in our interest and are not to our liking. By noticing them we can begin to decide whether we want to continue being caught up in them or not. Is anyone here interested in that skill?"

By doing this little bit of pantomime the teacher gets the attention of the audience and makes a teaching point about the nature of mindfulness.

Describing mindfulness as a skill

There are many advantages to describing mindfulness as a skill, as once it is acquired the client may choose to use it or not; for example, being able to drive a car does not prevent us from using public transport. A skill is also something that has to be learned and practised over time rather than something that can be done immediately. The idea of pacing and gradual shaping can help those clients who are prone to perfectionistic or unrealistic expectations. Learning mindfulness involves committing time and energy to attending sessions and then to practising at home. In the orientation phase we want to both alert the client to this requirement and motivate them to make the investment. In the following example Rachel is on an inpatient ward and expresses a certain amount of hostility to learning mindfulness.

> RACHEL. Oh, don't start all that 'mindfulness' rubbish again. I don't want to hear it.
>
> AVYAAN. Ah. Ok, that's awkward, because I was going to mention it and now, I can see that this is just going to be annoying. I certainly don't want to add to your problems, because I heard you have got a lot on your plate?
>
> RACHEL. You can say that again, I have a court case coming up, I'm not even supposed to be in here, I was supposed to be sent to a different hospital.
>
> AVYAAN. Oh no! And can they sort out the mix-up or are you stuck here now?

RACHEL. My doctor is onto it, I just have to wait, I am seeing her on Thursday.

AVYAAN. Ah, that's tough, it is a long time till Thursday, will you be able to forget it until then? Like, distract yourself?

RACHEL. Not much, because my family are closer to the other hospital. So, they can't get here every day.

AVYAAN. That's very painful, especially when other patients are having visitors.

RACHEL. It's horrid. Can't even smoke. But that's everywhere. They never let you anymore.

AVYAAN. That is a LOT of stuff to deal with.

RACHEL. Yes.

AVYAAN. Well, look, I'm not here to make your life worse. It's just this skill we could learn that might just help you get a few minutes respite from it all, because it doesn't seem fair that you have so much to carry all the time.

RACHEL. (Rolls her eyes) Oh, here we go, I should've known that was coming!

AVYAAN. (Laughs) No, no, it's not a trick, really – I honestly have just got this teeny skill that won't solve your whole life, but if you ever need to just turn the tap down on all that stuff going round and round in your mind... well... don't shoot the messenger, ok?

RACHEL. (Laughs, then sighs) Uh, what's the deal? Not raisins, is it?

AVYAAN. No raisins, and here's the deal, once you've learned it, you never have to do it UNLESS you want to. But if you don't learn it... well... what can I say?

RACHEL. (Sighs) I'm not promising...

AVYAAN. Me neither...

RACHEL. For God's sake. (Looks away) OK tell me when and all that.

The key here is that the therapist keeps the conversation light and friendly, drops the rope at the beginning so there is no tug of war, and looks for a way in which mindfulness will be helpful. Clients invariably have problems that monopolise their thinking and cause them distress. Giving people a way to get respite from the relentlessness of their worries is often an appealing gambit. Even when the therapist gets a grudging agreement from the client there is still no hard sell, by backing off and saying, "me neither" the therapist makes it more likely the client will come forward rather than back off. The therapist is not put off by the eye-rolling or sighing, just lays out the invitation in a way that is relevant to the client's difficulties.

Clients may already have associated mindfulness with Buddhism or eastern meditative practices. Even if they have not done so, it is not unusual for mindfulness leaders to start practices using a Tibetan singing bowl, which is a recognised symbol of eastern spirituality. In our experience there are mixed responses to the origins of mindfulness. For a number of clients, the fact that mindfulness has been practised for centuries makes it more appealing. They are deeply respectful of the cultural and spiritual background, valuing it over the scientific evidence. On the other hand, some clients are quite suspicious about the religious or foreign connections and consider it all 'a bit weird.' One client announced to the group that when he initially entered treatment, he was very uncertain about 'this voodoo stuff' but that it had turned out to be really helpful.

It is important at the outset to clarify that mindfulness is now being used as a practical skill in the treatment of mental health conditions, and to make reference to the research evidence. We have already highlighted some of the academic papers underpinning the growth in mindfulness-based therapies. If the client is curious, we can direct them to the evidence base or provide copies of relevant articles. People will often do their own investigations online. There are some informative videos on YouTube and a number of websites explaining both the origins and functions of mindfulness (there are some suggestions for recommended reading in Chapter 1 at the start of this book).

Occasionally, more often amongst other mindfulness teachers, we have encountered the view that the spiritual origins of mindfulness have been underplayed and that an eastern religion has been hijacked by western academics. We believe that the aim of the mindfulness teacher is not to overstate or understate either the spiritual or scientific components but to lay out factual information so that the client can make up their own mind.

In Chapter 1 we gave some definitions of mindfulness, and during the orientation phase it is useful to come back to some key phrases to act as reminders for the client. We do not want to get too wordy here as mindfulness is essentially an experiential phenomenon.

- 'Mindfulness means paying attention in a particular way: on purpose, in the present moment, and nonjudgmentally' (Kabat-Zinn, 1994: 4).

- Being mindful is the opposite of being absent-minded or on autopilot.

- Mindfulness is 'learning to be in control of your own mind instead of letting your mind be in control of you' (Linehan, 1993: 65).

Linking to the client's personal story

Whilst a 'sound bite' definition is handy for refocusing the client on the aim of mindfulness, most clients want the answer to the following question: "How will this help me with my problems?" The therapist is looking for a specific example to link the practice to the client's personal circumstances. Here is an example used in the orientation phase.

Lauren had a problem with overspending and was heavily in debt. On this particular occasion she had bought a coat that she could not really afford. Having brought it home she began to regret her purchase. The coat was still in the bag, unworn, and she had the receipt. The best thing to do, she decided, was to take it back to the shop. But when the time came her mind started to say, 'what if they don't believe you haven't worn it? What if it is the same girl who served you in the first place? She might challenge you, if anyone in the shop recognises you, they will think you are odd or stupid, they may guess that you're in debt; it will be embarrassing and horrid.' She began to feel her chest tighten and her stomach churn. So, she did not return the coat. Although this relieved her anxiety in the short term, now her level of debt is keeping her awake at night.

As an introduction to mindfulness her therapist said, "It looks like the actions of your mind prevented you from doing what you really wanted to do. Would it have been helpful if you could have unhooked from those thoughts in order to return your coat to the shop? But I can see how easy it was to get caught up in the content of your mind; those thoughts are very powerful. Mindfulness might help you to do more of the activities you really need to do. Have there been any other times when your mind stopped you doing something?"

Lauren went on to say that she had wanted to apply for a job but her mind kept saying that she'd never get work because no one would employ her.

In this case the therapist focused on an example that involved a clear objective, one that was within the client's capability, and where the only obstacle to reaching her goal was her response to the content of her mind. The therapist could have gone down the thought-challenging route, but in choosing mindfulness the teacher avoids an argument about whether the thoughts are true or not, and only needs to evaluate whether they helped Lauren get closer to her goal or pushed her away from it.

It's good practice for the teacher to then follow up with an example from her own life. Going on to provide a personal example can relay the message that the client's mind is not behaving oddly, that in fact everyone's mind behaves in a similar way. Here is an example that most people can relate to.

> When I am invited to a social event such as a party I usually say yes, thinking that it sounds nice, and as I get on well with the person who has invited me, it should be fun. But as the date draws closer my mind begins to follow a familiar track – it says, 'you might not actually like it, you've been so busy lately, you'll be tired, it will be a chore to get ready and go out, you'll have to stay till the end, people might not find you that interesting, it won't be much fun at all.' I then have an urge to ring up and give my apologies. If I am being unmindful, I will act on those urges. If I am mindful, however, I can identify that all of this content is just 'thought traffic' and I can unhook from it more easily. Needless to say, when I act opposite to my urges to avoid, I usually enjoy myself.

By sharing personal examples, the therapist acknowledges that we are all in the same boat, our minds are just doing what minds do.

During all mindfulness practices the therapist will do the exercises alongside the client and will feedback on out-of-session practice in the same way as the client. It is also important that, right from the start, we begin to use language that encourages the client to step back from the content of the mind. In this example we use the phrase 'thought traffic.' Another description we might have used is 'watching mind TV' to which one client memorably responded, "yes, and mine shows a lot of repeats."

Describing mindfulness using analogies

By now the client is perhaps beginning to think that mindfulness could have something to offer, and we can start to elaborate on the processes involved. We have found that clients respond well to analogies and here are our favourites: the first two are well-known metaphors that we've heard on courses and the second two we devised ourselves.

The spotlight of your attention

Imagine that your mind is like a huge spotlight, shining your attention onto a variety of objects throughout the day. We can't turn off the spotlight – it is always on; even when we are asleep it focuses on our dreams. But we can learn how to manoeuvre the spotlight around. We can move the spotlight of our attention to a focus of our own choosing, rather than leave the spotlight to shine randomly. The spotlight is often unwieldy and heavy to turn, and it may swing back when we try to move it. But gradually we can acquire the skill of moving it back to the most effective view. If you were trying to walk a tightrope in the dark, it would be more effective to illuminate the rope than the drop. If we are in a job interview it is more helpful to focus on answering the questions than remembering previous interviews that went badly.

The untrained puppy

Your mind is like an untrained puppy running around wherever it wants, following interesting smells, digging up your flower beds, burrowing under your fence. We can't train a puppy by just holding it still or putting it in a box. Instead, we need to notice where it has gone to and teach it to come back when we call. It will always wander off at times, but we can bring it under our control. As we start to exercise some control the puppy will still run off, and we have to be patient and gentle with it, being willing to call it back many times until it learns to respond more quickly to our command.

The radio receiver

Until I learned mindfulness, I used to believe that my mind was like a radio receiver: I would be forced to tune in on waking and then be stuck with whatever was being broadcast for the rest of the day. I had no idea that I could turn up the volume on some things, turn down the volume on others, and even change channels. In mindfulness we try to turn up the volume on the present moment and turn down the volume on the past or future. We can even learn to tune out distracting or unhelpful stimuli.

The mental muscle

We cannot stop our mind going off on thoughts that are not of our choosing. But when we notice it has gone and deliberately guide it back it is like exercising a mental muscle. So, if your mind wanders 20 times in the space of one minute, and you guide it back 20 times, you have done 20 units of exercise – like 20 press-ups for the mind. So, you do not need to worry if your mind wanders many times; every time you guide it back you enhance your mindfulness skill.

The most common response from clients to one of these analogies is to say, "My mind wanders off all the time." This is another opportunity for normalisation. A client might want to understand why their mind wanders so much, and especially to such negative content. The therapist can explain:

The role of the mind is to 'mind' you. That is, to look out for you to see that nothing goes wrong. Let's imagine that you are walking down the street with a friend. You might be fairly relaxed, picking out the things that are pleasing to look at. But if you were to employ that friend to 'mind' you, like a bodyguard, then your walk down the street might be very different. Perhaps they would guide you away from parked cars or hurry you through crowds, looking out for any place where danger could lurk. There would be no opportunity to chat. Your mind sometimes behaves this way, choosing to focus on insignificant things in case they portend danger. This made sense during evolution, when a rustle in the bushes might indicate an approaching predator, but it is not so help-ful now that there are fewer physical threats around. So, there is no need to criticise your mind for doing its job. Sometimes there is a need to protect you: when you're about to cross the road, or a mugger tries to grab your purse. You just need to notice what your mind is doing and realise that you don't always have to act on its advice. This is the same for all of us; our ancestors probably survived because our minds had the capacity to protect us this way.

In this explanation we are encouraging the client to have some curiosity about the actions of the mind, rather than judging it harshly.

Mindfulness is not meant to 'work'

We have just spent some time building a sense of optimism in the client that mindfulness might help with some of their dif-ficulties. So, it might seem odd to make a statement such as 'mindfulness is not meant to work.' Yet explaining this right at the beginning will help the therapist to avoid difficulties later on. It is quite a hard concept for both therapist and client to grasp; we are trying to unhook from expectation of what the current moment should deliver and to focus instead on experiencing it as it is. To focus on the end result can only take us away from the present moment.

The use of an analogy can help to get this message across. The common theme running through the following examples is that whilst the ultimate outcome might be desirable, the active pursuit of it will make it less likely to come about.

The argument

Let us imagine that you have fallen out with your friend, and you end up either shouting at each other or not speaking. Another friend, who cares about both of you, gives you some advice on how to patch things up: "You know, I think it would be really helpful if you were to spend some time just listening to her side of the story. It might just help to take some heat out of the situation, and then perhaps both of you will calm down."

You reply, "Do you think so? OK, that sounds like a good idea because I really want her to stop going on about this issue. So how long do you think I should spend listening? Would 30 minutes do it? Or maybe an hour? Or do you think it should be longer? I need to know how long I have got to listen before she stops going on about this. Just tell me how many minutes you think it will take. I'll do it. It'll be worth it."

Clearly anyone going into a discussion with this attitude is not really going to listen very well at all. They are far too focused on how many minutes it will take and on getting the outcome they want. But even if this person does listen mindfully there are no guarantees that the argument will subside. If you go into mindfulness looking for a specific outcome it will prevent you from being fully present in the moment.

The first date

It is perfectly reasonable that someone might want to eventually get married and have a family. But most people recognise the danger of starting a first date with this outcome in mind. Once again, being focused on a desired outcome would take you away from experiencing the true relationship. But even being fully present in each moment of the first date will not guarantee that this will be your life partner.

The soufflé

What happens if you are cooking a soufflé or a cake and keep opening the oven door to check if it is cooked? The dish never rises. The action of checking alters the course of events by lowering the temperature inside the oven. The more you check, the lower the temperature. But even accomplished cooks who keep that oven door shut will sometimes experience a fallen soufflé.

It is hard for any of us to engage in activity without targets, expectations or guarantees. Devoting some time to providing this explanation during the orientation phase is well worth the effort. Later on, if the client says after a practice "I did the exercise but it didn't work," the therapist can then gently remind them that mindfulness is not meant to 'work' without having to re-engage in protracted discussion. This seemingly paradoxical phrase can act as a cue, unhooking the client from their attachment to outcome. The therapist needs to beware, however, that without the initial explanation this response can sound trite or glib.

There are many other things that mindfulness will not do for us. It will not stop our mind from wandering – only help us to notice that it has wandered and teach us how to guide it back. It is not relaxation – in fact, we go to great lengths to distinguish between mindfulness and relaxation as we will see in the next chapter. It will not turn us into 'good' people. The central message is this: in mindfulness we are not trying to get anywhere, we are trying to be somewhere, in the here and now. During supervision of practitioners, we have sometimes heard them say: "My client doesn't want to learn mindfulness because they have done it already." This implies the client has not understood the 'being' aspect of mindfulness, viewing it instead like a course that just needs to be completed for lasting benefit to occur.

Mindfulness in everyday life

When we learn any new skill, we have to transfer our ability to use that skill from the learning environment into the real world. The aim of teaching mindfulness skills is not to turn clients into meditators, or to teach them to be mindful only in the presence of a therapist in a quiet room prompted by the sound of a bell. The ultimate goal is that clients will be able to be mindful at home, at work, out socialising or undertaking solitary activities. In short, it is to be able to lead their lives more mindfully.

Clients should be alerted to the need to undertake homework assignments and to feedback how they are getting on with practising at home. It may be helpful to suggest keeping a log of their practice (as described in *Using Mindfulness Sills in Everyday Life: A Practical Guide*; Dunkley and Stanton, 2016). The therapist will also describe their own use of mindfulness out of session, both formally, such as setting aside specific time to do sitting practices, and informally, through being mindful in different situations. The following examples come from both clients and therapists and can be used to illustrate how mindfulness is incorporated into everyday life.

Focusing attention on the present

"I had to travel to my sister's house which is 20 miles away. Usually, I would be fretting about it all week so that by the time I actually set off I felt like I'd been travelling for hours! This week I reminded myself; I'm not doing the journey right now, it's not until Wednesday."

"Whenever I took my kids to the park, I used to dread telling them when it was time to go home. I would think about how upset and grumpy they would become. It used to put me off taking them. Now I am mindful of what we are doing when we are in the park. They still kick up a fuss when we leave but it doesn't spoil the whole afternoon."

Increasing awareness

"I never used to notice when I was getting tense at work. Now I am more mindful of my posture, and my body tells me when I need to walk and stretch. My neck is much less painful."

"If I was eating, I would always be doing something else at the same time: reading the paper, watching TV, chatting, planning what to do with my day. Now I focus on the food as it goes into my mouth and experience the taste and texture. I enjoy my food more."

"I knocked over a carton of orange juice and my mind said immediately, 'That was stupid.' In the past I would have got really upset but I said to myself, 'That's a judgement' and set about clearing it up mindfully – focusing on the feel of the cloth and the sight of the sponge soaking up the juice."

Being effective

"I could never talk to my husband about money without it turning into a row. Now I am mindful of choosing a time when we're not tired, and I describe the situation mindfully without making lots of judgements. As a result, we've been able to make proper decisions about how to solve the problem."

"I would avoid telling my friends that my birthday was coming up; I used to think that they should remember. Then I was upset when they forgot and so were they. I now realise that just wasn't effective; I am much more mindful of doing what works – I send an email asking if people want to come out for my birthday."

An effective mindfulness teacher is always collecting examples to illustrate these conceptual points, each of which will be expanded in the following chapters. Of course, examples from past clients are even more effective when told in person. In our

NHS trust we were fortunate to have two service-user groups, where past clients become teaching colleagues, helping to orient new clients. Having access to someone who has been through the treatment is invaluable, and newcomers often report feeling inspired by people who have overcome their own difficulties through using mindfulness techniques.

There will still be some situations in which others believe mindfulness is exactly what the client needs but the client, despite having received all the information, simply does not agree. No matter how skilful the orientation, it is the client who makes the final decision as to whether they wish to proceed, and mindfulness does not appeal to everyone. In these circumstances it is the mindfulness teacher who needs to gently let go of the attachment.

Key tasks

- Describe mindfulness as a skill.
- Provide access to the literature and other media.
- Validate the client's concerns.
- Link to the client's goals and use client-specific examples.
- Elaborate on what's involved in mindfulness using analogies.
- Explain what mindfulness is not going to do.
- Highlight the objective of living everyday life more mindfully.

Stylistic factors

- Model mindful acceptance of the client's responses.
- Unhook from our own attachment to outcome.
- Use examples, analogies and stories where possible.
- Be honest about limitations.

- Involve past practitioners.
- Use personal examples to indicate that we are all in the same boat.
- Model curiosity about the actions of the mind.
- Keep a lightness of touch.

Bibliography

Dunkley, C. and Stanton, M., 2016. *Using Mindfulness Skills in Everyday Life: A Practical Guide*. Routledge.

Kabat-Zinn, J., 1994. *Wherever You Go, There You Are: Mindfulness Meditation for Everyday Life*. Piatkus Books.

Linehan, M., 1993. *Cognitive-Behavioral Treatment of Borderline Personality Disorder*. Guilford Press.

Introducing a mindfulness practice

In this chapter we will outline how to introduce a mindfulness exercise to someone who is completely new to this concept, including instructions for setting up the practice and some pointers for the mindfulness teacher. Chapter 4 will then describe how to take feedback after an exercise in order to maximise client learning.

The function of a practice exercise

In Chapter 2 we outlined how to present the idea of mindfulness in a way that makes it appealing to the client. We described linking mindfulness to their long-term goals and highlighting situations from their daily life in which this skill would be helpful. The next stage is to move into conducting a practice. This serves a number of functions:

- The client gets to practise the action of deliberately focusing their attention (exercising the 'mental muscle').

- The client practises accepting the current experience with kind curiosity ('being' in the moment).

- The client learns to identify the components of an experience (expanding awareness).

DOI: 10.4324/9781003386117-3

- The client learns to identify obstacles to mindfulness (the antics of the 'untrained puppy,' see Chapter 2).
- The client is encouraged to generalise the skill from the therapy room to everyday life (the 'take-home' message, see Chapter 8).

Tell a story to introduce the concept of mindfulness

Even if people are familiar with the concept of mindfulness, at the start of a session or exercise it is sometimes nice to ease in with a personal story. It engages your client and paves the way for the practice that is to come. Here are some examples:

> The other day I was watching some children in the park playing with bubbles. I noticed that I would watch one of the bubbles that floated near, until it burst, and then I would be attracted to another. In some ways this is like our thoughts, they bubble up and occupy space in the forefront of our mind, and then they go, another one taking their place. Sometimes there are lots of them, competing for our attention. Today we are going to learn that we can choose which thought bubbles to follow, or decide to turn our mind away to something else.
>
> In our GP surgery waiting room is a huge fish tank. When I am in there I am mesmerised by the fish. Each seems to come to the front of the tank, and then retreat to the rear. I prefer the colourful ones to the muddy brown ones, and get disappointed when the brighter fish go to the back. This is like our minds attaching to certain thoughts and pushing away others. Today we are going to learn how to notice our thoughts rather than get attached to them.

> At the supermarket I frequently end up wandering past the items I need, only noticing when I get home that I forgot the onions or the shampoo. Today we are going to learn how to live our lives more mindfully, so that we don't miss those things we want to pay attention to.

Keep it simple

Practices can be completely spontaneous. Here is an example that a therapist might give either in individual therapy or in a group, without much preparation.

> Right now, in this moment, run your finger lightly from the tip of your index finger down through the palm of your hand and onto your wrist. What did you notice? Was there a sensation? Is it still there? Did your mind wander off when you did that? Where did it go? Into the future: 'I could do this with a client'? Or into the past: 'I remember doing this exercise before'? Or did it stay on the sensation? Were you judging yourself: 'I don't think I'm doing this right?' Or were you judging the exercise: 'How can this help anyone? This is rubbish'?

In this instance there was very little setup and the stimulus was – pardon the pun – ready to hand. But it contained the most essential ingredients of a practice: there was a chosen focus for the attention; and there was some guidance to help the client expand awareness.

However, if we have a little time, we can add some ingredients that make our practice even more effective, although the ultimate aim *is* to be spontaneously mindful. In our experience of training therapists, the most difficult challenge is to keep things simple. Therapists often have the urge to get very wordy and intellectual, and occasionally might say, "This is all too basic for me. I need something much more advanced." This is missing the point. Mindfulness is not about the highlights – it is about the spaces in between. When we seek to add complexity, we are rejecting the current experience, wanting it to be something other than it is. A truly advanced practitioner approaches every task as though it is the first time it has ever been done. We may conduct the same breathing practice hundreds of times, but the art is to be as alive and awake the first time as the last. The real skill is to open ourselves fully to the moment, whatever it contains.

Getting ready for the practice

Our first instruction to the client will often relate to posture. Right from the outset we want to be very clear about the difference between mindfulness and relaxation. It can be difficult for both clients and therapists to unhook from the notion that the client should feel calm or relaxed at the end of the practice. It becomes even more complicated when practising mindfulness of the breath, as clients may have done anxiety management groups where there has been a focus on deep breathing to induce a relaxed state. For this reason, instead of saying 'sit comfortably' we prefer the instruction to sit in a dignified position. We advise the client to place both feet on the floor and keep their back upright, if they are able. We are doing the opposite of relaxation – reminding our body that we want it to be alert and alive. We have been asked about encouraging clients to adopt the lotus position or to sit on the floor. This can be very helpful at one level – acting as a 'cue' to the body that we are about to engage in a practice. On the other hand, it is less likely to be practised in a variety of situations, at home or at work. We want clients to practise on the bus, in the waiting room at the dentist and at the dinner table. Our advice is to vary positions over time, but stack the deck in favour of those with most day-to-day utility.

We are also going to ask our clients to try to keep their eyes open. Again, if people have been used to relaxation classes, they may find this odd. Also, if they are trying to concentrate, they may find it easier to do so by shutting out any visual distractions. We explain this request by reminding clients that the function of mindfulness is to help us in our day-to-day life. In the example from Chapter 2, Lauren would not have been able to return the coat to the shop with her eyes closed. However, especially in a group situation, it is not worth getting into a tug of war with clients, so if they want to close their eyes, they can, but encourage them to work towards keeping them open in future practices. We will come back to this issue in Chapter 4, which is on taking feedback after the practice. For those who are willing to practise with their eyes open, you can advise them to just find a place for their eyes to rest that might not be too distracting, perhaps a spot on the floor or on the table in front of them. It can be helpful not to look at any written words as our minds tend to start reading what we see. Many people find it easier if they angle their eyes slightly downwards, as the action of staring into space straight ahead, or upwards, is a posture often associated with daydreaming. Again, the ultimate aim is to be able to be mindful in any position.

Finally, the therapist needs to ensure that they do not conduct the practice in what we term 'therapist voice.' This phenomenon occurs when the therapist changes their timbre and tone from their usual speaking voice, just as some people have a 'telephone voice.' When leading mindfulness the therapist may have a subconscious urge to soften their tone, slow their voice down or become more melodic. Unfortunately these changes give the subtle impression that we are now going to *r... e... l... a... a... a... x... x... x.* The therapist may have to make a conscious effort to retain a normal tone of voice.

Give clear instructions

Whatever focus you are going to choose for a mindfulness exercise, there are some key points that you need to get across to the client before you start. Below is a generic script that we have used in mindfulness groups.

> We are going to do a mindfulness practice. During this exercise I will guide you to focus on a particular item or experience. As you are following the instructions your mind is likely to wander to other things. This is perfectly normal. When you notice that your mind has wandered, gently return it to the task. Do this as many times as you need to. When you do this, you are being mindful.

The key points are:

- We have a specific focus for our attention.
- It is normal for your mind to wander.
- What to do if it does wander.
- You may have to repeat the same action again and again.
- Despite your mind wandering, if you *return it*, you have been mindful.

If you have a DBT group or longstanding mindfulness group you may eventually have more experienced clients leading a practice, and it is helpful to have these instructions for them to read at the start.

Indicating the start and end of the exercise

There has been a degree of debate on the use of a 'singing bowl' or 'mindfulness bell' to begin and end a practice. For some people the bell has religious connotations so it is wise to have a very flexible approach to starting and ending practices. The bell is simply used as a cue, and the therapist is encouraged to use a variety of cues. Here are a few we have used: tapping a tea-spoon against a glass; tapping the table with a pencil; saying 'start' and 'stop'; raising a hand to indicate the start and end; or just beginning the exercise (for example, if we are mindfully listening to a piece of music). We want to discourage the client from imagining that mindfulness is only done under very special circumstances. For the same reason we do not want to put a note on the door saying 'quiet please, mindfulness group in progress.' The more normal the conditions under which clients learn the skill, the easier it will be for them to generalise it into their everyday life.

Duration of a practice

Mindfulness practices can be anything from one minute long to a number of hours. Our experience is that clients find it easier to begin with shorter practices, but we hope that therapists will again be flexible in their approach, assessing and attending to both the needs of the client and their theoretical model. Both clients and therapists will benefit from building up the length of their practice over time. We have noticed in our own practice that we can get complacent at the ease of practice with short exercises and assume that a longer practice is just 'more of the same.' But this is not the case, and regular extended practice for the therapist will enhance their competence to teach and model the skill.

Having said this, many clients have very intense experiences of their internal environment. They may use substances or self-harm as a way of avoiding their thoughts, images and sensations. For these clients a two- or three-minute practice is a long time. Our advice is to keep those early practices short. For similar reasons it is advisable to start with an exercise that focuses on something quite tangible that is outside of the client. In the remainder of this chapter, we will outline some simple exercises of external stimuli, and then in Chapter 5 we will move onto mindfulness of internal experiences. We are including scripts that can be used to lead a practice as a helpful learning tool for the therapist but we would dissuade therapists from always relying on a script as this can inhibit authentic experiencing. Over time the therapist will become comfortable with introducing the practices without the script. Again, variety and flexibility are the key.

Mindfulness of sounds

In this practice we are going to be mindful of sounds. If you are able, then try and keep your eyes open, just find a place for them to rest. The task is simply to notice sounds that we hear. We are not attempting to label the sounds, although this might automatically happen. Our minds have been used to labelling sounds so it is likely that as we hear 'tick tock' our minds may say, 'that's the clock.' Or if we hear 'dringg dringg' our minds may say, 'that's a phone.' If this happens then there is no need to judge your mind for doing what it has always done; instead, just gently guide it back to the next sound. Whatever your mind starts to do, even if it goes into stories or memories associated with the sounds, the skill is just to bring it back to the next sound. Do this as many times as you need to until I signal the end of the exercise.

This exercise would typically run for two or three minutes after which the therapist would take feedback (see Chapter 4).

The skill that the therapist is teaching during this 'mindfulness of sounds' is that of 'observing,' i.e., noticing without having to put words to the experience. Marsha Linehan (2015a, 2015b) describes the three 'What Skills' of mindfulness: 'observe, describe and participate.' She urges the mindfulness teacher to be very clear on which of these 'What Skills' is being practised, as they should be done one at a time. A classic mistake of therapists who are new to leading a practice is to give additional instructions such as "If you have a judgement just label it and imagine it as a cloud in the sky floating by, then bring your mind back to the sound." The client then becomes very confused about what they are meant to be doing, are they supposed to be labelling their thoughts? Are they to conjure up new images? The most effective practices allow the client to rehearse one skill at a time.

In our example exercise 'mindfulness of sounds' the therapist gave all the instructions at the start of the exercise and then remained silent until the practice was over. The therapist usually joins in with the exercise: remaining silent, modelling a mindful posture and not responding to distractions in the room. Do not worry about repeating the same exercise many times. Repetition allows clients to notice changes between the first time they practised and more recent occasions. Listening mindfully is also a skill that can be practised in any location.

A client recounted keeping a bedside vigil when her sister was seriously ill in hospital. She found that her mind constantly wandered into the future (fears that her sister would not recover) and into the past (the accident that had caused her sister to be admitted). She found she could not concentrate enough to read, and there were a number of other ill patients in the ward so talking or watching TV was discouraged. She turned her attention to being mindful of sound. At first she became alarmed, adding a label to each sound she heard, trying to work out whether it was good news or bad news (the sound of footsteps approaching: good or bad? A click from the monitor: good or bad?) But over time she became more effective at just receiving the sensation of each hum, swish, click or whoosh that she heard, attaching to none and pushing away none. She found that her own body sounds – her breathing, the creak of her chair as she moved position – became part of the experience of sound. Did mindfulness turn this experience into one that was pleasant? No. Did it make the time pass more quickly? No, but she stopped adding to her own distress by recalling the past or predicting the future. She found that she was able to tolerate the present moment more easily.

Guided mindfulness of an object

This is a different type of exercise, one in which the therapist gives instructions throughout the practice. For this example, we have chosen to be mindful of a leaf. This is one of our favourite exercises as we worked in the NHS and leaves are cheap. If the exercise is being practised in a group, then, as the therapist invites the clients to choose a leaf, there is an opportunity to make a very useful teaching point:

I can see all of you reaching to select a leaf, and I want you to raise your hand if you had the thought 'I want a good leaf.' The interesting thing is that, for each of you, what would constitute a 'good leaf' is different (the therapist can now ask some of the participants what they thought would make a 'good leaf,' typical answers are "One that is completely free from blemishes or indentations" or "One that is different from the others in form or colour." Or "The biggest!" Which usually gets a laugh. How interesting it is that even if you have never done this exercise before your mind already has a protocol for it. It gets out the file labelled 'a list of qualities for a "good leaf" for a situation in which you are asked to observe one during a mindfulness practice.' It is not just this current situation in which your mind has an agenda. It has millions of these protocols, producing them at the drop of a hat. Also, it won't wait for you to request the protocol, it will just hand it to you as *though these are the rules*. In mindfulness we learn to notice when this happens and then to exercise choice. We can choose to follow the protocol or we can choose to ignore it.

The therapist can then move on to give further orientation to the exercise, alerting clients to the fact that on this occasion they will continue to give verbal prompts throughout the practice. The aim of this practice is to ensure that the client uses a variety of senses to experience the object. Guided exercises can be helpful if clients are new to the technique, as the therapist takes responsibility for moving the focus of attention from one experience to another. The knack of pacing the exercise is to allow the client time to linger a little over each separate question, pausing before moving onto the next focus.

During this practice I shall guide you through a series of observations. If your mind wanders, then gently bring it back to the leaf and follow the next instruction.

- First of all, hold the leaf in the palm of your hand. Notice the weight of it. How does it feel against the skin on your palm? Are there places where it touches and places where it doesn't?

- Pick it up between your fingers and thumb. Notice the temperature of the leaf: does it feel warm or cool? Is it the same temperature all over? Does the temperature change as you hold it between your fingers?

- Notice the texture of the leaf: does it feel rough or smooth? Do the edges of the leaf feel the same as the centre? Is it hard or soft, firm or limp to the touch, damp or dry? Does the stalk feel the same?

- Allow your eye to follow the contour of the leaf. Notice its shape and size. View it from a variety of angles and see the shape change in your eyeline. How thin is it? How wide at its widest point?

- Notice the colour on the upper side of the leaf. See any variations in shade and texture. Look at the detailing: any veins, ridges, patterns? Explore every part of the leaf, the edges, the middle, the stalk.

- Now taking the leaf in your fingers turn it over and notice how the underside differs in colour and texture. Notice how the light catches the leaf differently as you move it.

- Is there a smell to the leaf? Is it more evident towards the stalk or in the body of the leaf, does it change if you run your nail over the leaf?

- Continue to use your senses to observe the leaf until I ring the bell to signal the end of the exercise.

Any object can be used for this type of mindfulness practice. Items that are commonly encountered around the home act as an additional prompt to the client to generalise the skill. Here are a few other suggestions for items that won't break the budget:

> stones, shells, crystals, acorns, pine cones, conkers, twigs, feathers, wheat stalks, flowers, fruit, vegetables, water, raisins, biscuits, dried pasta (spaghetti is a particular favourite for its projectile snapping qualities), cinnamon sticks, sweets (those in a wrapper offer additional opportunities to be mindful), tea bags, pieces of fabric, cotton wool, sponge, pictures from magazines or birthday cards, keys, buttons, stamps, coins, beads, toothbrushes, string, ornaments (particularly small models of animals that can be picked up for a few pence at charity shops), marbles and coloured pencils.

Mindfulness of the breath

Mindfulness of the breath is a universally recognised practice, but it can be hard for patients who have suffered from anxiety. Noticing the rate of their breathing can be the cue that sets off a panic attack. A number of clients may resist this exercise or experience discomfort during it, so it is not the best choice for the client's first mindfulness practice. However, paradoxically it can also be the most useful of all mindfulness practices. The breath is always accessible, readily available at any time of the day or night.

This is the script for a mindfulness exercise that we have used regularly with clients. There are two features of the script that we have found useful with clients who have anxiety. One is that it begins by directing the focus outside of the body and moves the attention slowly inwards towards the breath. The other is that it adds an instruction to label the 'in' and 'out' breaths. These factors seem to have reduced the number of people reporting anxiety symptoms.

Just take a moment to arrive here in this room. Allow the walls of the room to act as a barrier, keeping out whatever happened before you came into this room, keeping out whatever might happen after you leave.

Let's bring our attention to the way we are connected to this room, moving the spotlight of our mind to the very soles of our feet. Can you sense the hardness of the floor beneath your shoes? And now pay all of your attention to the sensation of being seated on the chair. Notice how it feels to allow your weight to rest on the chair, feel the sensation on your legs and your bottom and your back as the chair holds you up.

And now bring your attention in further to notice that you are breathing. We're not attempting to alter the rate of our breathing in any way, but if it does alter, that's fine, just notice without judging. Bring the spotlight of your mind to the point in your body where you are most aware of your breath. This may be in your nostrils, or in the rise and fall of your chest, or in the expansion and contraction of your abdomen. Wherever that place is for you, see if you can tell the difference between the in-breath and the out-breath.

Notice that every in-breath is followed by an out-breath, and every out-breath is followed by an in-breath. Notice the point at which your breath changes from going in to coming out. If your mind wanders, then gently guide it back to the in-breath or the out-breath.

Now as my voice falls away continue to focus on the breath. It may help you as you are breathing in to say quietly in your mind, 'IN,' and as you are breathing out to say quietly in your mind, 'OUT.' Continue to do this until I signal the end of the exercise.

This exercise may still occasionally result in a client having some kind of panic response, and advice will be given in Chapter 4 on what to do if this happens. Our advice to the teacher is not to be put off doing the practice by the occasional adverse reaction or negative comment. This particular exercise is still one of the most useful, and objections (the client's and the therapist's) often fall away with practice. Learning to accept the breath however it comes is more beneficial to patients than trying to avoid being aware of it, as the breath is with us at all times whether we like it or not.

Mindful body scan

Another universally recognised practice is the body scan, and there are numerous examples available in books and recordings. The idea is to move the client's focus around the body. This has proved very effective for clients who are suffering from physical pain. Recurrent pain in one part of the body – back or shoulder, for example – will often draw the attention to the exclusion of everything else. This increased awareness can heighten the sensation of pain. One of our clients with post-operative pain told us that he used the body scan practice on a daily basis, describing the effect as 'diluting the sensations of pain.'

A further reason for practising the body scan is that our experience of the world comes through our body. Some clients have very little awareness of their physical self, and therapists are familiar with the client who is 'stuck in their head,' cut off from their body sensations. The body scan can be a form of exposure to genuine physical experiencing. This is a concept to which we will return in later chapters.

The body scan can be contracted or expanded but we usually start with 15 minutes and build up as the client's skill increases. Some mindfulness teachers ask their clients to bring a mat and lie on the floor. We conduct our practices with clients sitting in a chair as this is the posture they are more than likely going to adopt when they are using the skill outside of the mindfulness room.

Again, we advise you to leave a short pause at the end of each sentence.

Doing a mindfulness body scan can be like being in a scanning machine, except that instead of radio waves we are using our own attention to scan our body. While we are doing this practice, if you notice that your mind gets preoccupied by one part of your body, perhaps because there is pain or discomfort, then just try to treat that part as you do all the others: don't avoid it and don't linger there as the practice moves on. Just listen for the next instruction.

- Let's start by bringing that attention to our scalp, right at the crown of our head. Can you feel the skin across your forehead?
- Perhaps you have the sensation of hair touching your ears or the back of your neck.
- Can you feel any sensation in your eyes? And now in your cheeks?
- Notice the feeling in your lower jaw: perhaps it is tightly closed, or a little open. Bring your attention slowly downwards, over your chin and onto your neck.
- Notice the front of your neck, with the breath going up and down your throat, and the hollow of your collarbone. Scan round and up the back of your neck, feeling your head resting at the top of your spine.
- Now move your attention to scan the top of your shoulders, noticing if they are high, up under your ears or if they are hunched forward or sloping down towards your arms.

- Move your attention to your arms, down to the elbows, then down your forearm to the wrist. Can you move your attention all the way round the bracelet of each wrist? How does it feel?

- Now push your attention all the way through your hand to the very tips of your fingers and your thumbs. Can you feel any pulse in those thumbs?

- Now notice your upper body, your ribcage and chest. Do you have any sensation there? In your mind, follow the sensation down your breastbone to the softness of the abdomen beneath. Notice the sensation down each of the little bones in your back, from your neck down to your waist. Can you scan around the girdle of your waist?

- Notice the feeling of your hips and upper thighs. Feel your weight being supported by your bottom on the chair.

- Follow the line of your thighs down to your knees. Can you feel the chair beneath you? Is the temperature different on the back of your thighs to the front?

- Bring your attention over the curve of your knees. Can you feel the hardness of your kneecap? Can you feel the skin over the top? Now notice the angle of your shins and calves as you bring your attention down towards your ankles.

- Are you aware of any sensations in your heels, perhaps you can feel the cradle of your shoe around them? Notice the soles of your feet, and slowly drive your awareness to the very end of your toes, noticing the little toes on each foot and then your big toes. Notice if you have any feeling in the very tips of those big toes.

Notice that the teacher does not instruct the client to change anything that they notice in their body. For example, although the client's attention may be drawn to tension, perhaps in the jaw or the shoulders, there is no suggestion that they relax their jaw or loosen their shoulders. This is another difference between mindfulness and relaxation. In mindfulness we accept what's there.

Mindfulness of an action or activity

These practices fall into two categories. One type is activities that we might normally do, but mindlessly rather than with our full attention. For example, we might practice mindfully rising from sitting to standing, feeling our centre of gravity change, and noticing all the muscles involved to bring us into an upright position. Or we might fold a piece of paper and put it into an envelope, mindfully. This would mean paying attention to the temperature of the paper, the thinness of its edge, the way the crease forms as we run our finger along the fold. The smell of the sealant on the open edge of the envelope, the sensation of the different kinds of paper sliding over each other. In one of our exercises, we got clients to write themselves a note urging themselves to be mindful in everyday life, and place it in an envelope, which they then addressed to themselves. We then posted them and a few days later they received their notes, reinforcing the message that mindfulness is for life and not just the classroom.

The second kind of activity practice is some type of action you might not normally undertake. For example, rubbing your tummy and patting your head at the same time, or throwing a ball of wool to each other across the circle whilst keeping hold of the loose end, creating a spider's web of strands across the middle. We might pour sand into a tray and invite people to make patterns in it. Or give people a selection of stones with which to build a tower.

We will give more examples of mindful activity in Chapter 6, as it relates strongly to being mindful in everyday life. As you build your repertoire of practices the idea is to vary them as much as you can. The more mindful activities you invite your clients to do, the more likely they will be to carry on their practice when you're not with them. Encouraging them to keep a log of their practice can also help them to continue with this outside of sessions as detailed in the client guide that accompanies this book (Dunkley and Stanton, 2016).

In this chapter we have described how to set up an exercise, and given examples of some common practices. In Chapter 4 we will describe how the therapist takes feedback from the exercises and deals with the comments from both enthusiastic clients and those who are more ambivalent.

Key tasks

- Keep it simple.
- Clearly define the focus of attention.
- Restrict instructions for the practice to 'one thing at a time.'
- Give guidance on what to do if the mind wanders off the task.
- Vary the length of practice according to the client's experience level.
- Participate in the exercise with the client.

Stylistic factors

- Avoid using 'therapist voice.'
- Make clear that mindfulness is not relaxation.
- Moderate the pace of your instructions.

- Vary the length of practice according to client experience.
- Provide both variety and repetition when choosing exercises.
- Include practices that generalise easily to everyday life.
- Avoid creating 'special conditions' (e.g., lighting) in case the client assumes this is a prerequisite for practice.

Bibliography

Dunkley, C. and Stanton, M., 2016. *Using Mindfulness Skills in Everyday Life: A Practical Guide*. Routledge.

Linehan, M., 2015a. *DBT Skills Training Manual*. Guilford Press.

Linehan, M., 2015b. *DBT Skills Training Handouts and Worksheets*. Guilford Press.

CHAPTER 4

Taking feedback after a mindfulness practice

In Chapter 3 we described how to conduct some simple mindfulness exercises. Now we are moving on to the stage of taking feedback from the client when the practice has ended. This is a chance for the therapist to hone and refine the client's skill of being awake to their internal environment.

The function of feedback is to:

- gather information about the client's current skill level
- highlight both mindful and unmindful behaviour of the client
- identify any obstacles that prevent the client from being mindful
- problem-solve obstacles
- shape the client's awareness of their mind's activities
- help the client to generalise the skill from the therapy room to their natural environment.

Immediately after a mindfulness exercise the therapist invites the client to share some observations. A question such as "What did you notice?" or "What came up for you during that practice?" is preferable to "How did you find that?" as the latter will often prompt evaluative responses such as "That was lovely" or "It

DOI: 10.4324/9781003386117-4

was horrid." If the therapist also gets caught up in the evaluation of the practice as either 'good' or 'bad' they might miss the chance to shape the client's skill. There are three components of mindfulness that can be shaped during feedback, which might be referred to as the three A's: Attention, Awareness and Acceptance.

Attention control

This is the skill of focusing on one stimulus in the present moment, bringing the mind back repeatedly despite distractions from either the internal or external environment. Here are some examples of the sort of questions that would help strengthen this particular skill.

- Did your mind wander during the practice?
- Did you notice that it had drifted off?
- Did you bring it back to the focus?
- Did you have to do that many times?
- Did you get caught up in the thoughts and experiences that pulled you away from the focus?
- How long do you think it was till you realised you were thinking about something else?
- What helped you to get back to the task?

Being able to turn the focus of attention away from unwanted intrusions is the key to managing unpleasant memories, flashbacks, images, auditory hallucinations, worry thoughts or other internal phenomena. It is also useful for clients who have to tolerate noisy, risky or emotionally charged environments without rising to provocation.

Awareness of internal experiences

This second feature of mindfulness is learning to identify and label the different components of an experience: types of thoughts, emotions, sensations and urges. Just as an English grammar teacher may help a student label the parts of speech, the therapist helps the client identify the activities of the mind. This shapes the client's ability to observe the transient nature of their mind's content. In Chapter 5 we elaborate further on the different kinds of thought such as judgements, assumptions and interpretations.

In this example the therapist, Tina, takes feedback from the client, Joan, after a group exercise.

TINA.   We have just been mindful of a pine cone, and I talked you through some prompts to help bring your mind back when it wanders off. I'm just wondering what you noticed during the exercise? (Therapist invites some reflections on the practice using open questions.)

JOAN.   My mind was all over the place.

TINA.   OK, so you noticed that your mind had gone on to something else; that was mindful of you. Did you only realise it had done that after we finished, or were you aware of it at the time? (Therapist highlights that the client has managed some mindfulness, and checks out the level of skill deployed during the exercise.)

JOAN.   Er, at the time, I thought, I need to focus on the cone, but it was hard.

TINA.   It is a really difficult skill to master; that's why we do so much practice. Tell me, what got your mind back to the cone? (Therapist validates the difficulty of the task and checks out what cued the client back into being mindful.)

JOAN.   When you said about the colours, because I noticed mine has got black on it, like it's been scorched or something.

TINA.   So, using your senses – listening to my voice and looking at the cone – was helpful in bringing your mind back. And you made an interpretation about it having been scorched. Did anything else happen as a result of that thought, like an urge, or a sensation, or an emotion? (Therapist summarises factors that promoted mindfulness and labels an 'interpretation.' She then draws the client's attention to consequences.)

JOAN.   I had the urge to look at everyone else's cone to see if theirs were black.

TINA.   And did you act on that urge or ignore it? (Therapist highlights two possible options in response to an urge.)

JOAN.   I didn't look round in case people thought, 'What's she gawping at?'

TINA.   What happened to the urge, did it go up, go down or stay the same? (Therapist ignores the content of this particular thought in the interest of making a teaching point about urges.)

JOAN.   (Ponders.) I guess it must have gone down because I started to think about something else then, about when we were at school and we used to spray pine cones white for Christmas.

TINA.   Sounds like your mind got distracted by an association with other pine cones that you have held in the past. It's interesting how our minds work that way and how quickly we can get engrossed in a memory. So, have we discovered anything about urges during that practice? (Therapist uses the label 'association' and then pulls for some evidence of learning from the client.)

JOAN.   That they can go away even if you don't act on them.

During this brief exchange Tina was enhancing the client's skill by labelling different mental phenomena and highlighting when the client was being mindful. She chose to raise Joan's awareness of urges, perhaps because Joan is trying to reduce an unwanted behaviour, such as smoking, self-harming or binge-eating. She helps Joan to recognise that an urge can reduce without having to act on it.

However, if there is a more helpful learning point, the therapist might pursue a different line of enquiry. Here is another possible example from the same scenario.

TINA.   So, using your senses – listening to my voice and looking at the cone – was helpful in bringing your mind back. And you made an interpretation about it having been scorched. Did anything else happen as a result of that thought, like an urge, or a sensation, or an emotion? (Therapist summarises factors that promoted mindfulness and labels an 'interpretation.' She then draws the client's attention to consequences.)

JOAN.   I had the urge to look at everyone else's cone to see if theirs were black.

TINA.   That's interesting. Did you notice any emotion around when you had that urge? (Therapist models gentle curiosity.)

JOAN.   I guess I was feeling anxious, like there was something wrong with my cone.

TINA.   So, you had the emotion of anxiety and then had an urge to make comparisons. Were you aware of making the decision to do that? (Therapist summarises and then refocuses the client's attention on the process, pulling for more awareness.)

JOAN.   No, it just kind of happened automatically.

TINA.   It's amazing how quickly we go from an emotion to an action without really noticing. Does that ever happen outside of here? That you feel anxious and then have urges to compare yourself with other people? (Therapist links in-session awareness to out-of-session events.)

JOAN.   (Laughs.) All the time!

TINA.   And is making comparisons usually effective for you? (Therapist encourages the client to be mindful of consequences.)

JOAN.   Hardly ever, it usually makes me more anxious.

TINA.   So, what could you do next time you notice the emotion of anxiety and the urge to make comparisons? (Therapist restates the mindful descriptions of internal phenomena.)

JOAN   I'm not sure.

TINA.   You could just describe it mindfully, 'I notice I am having the emotion of anxiety' and 'I notice I am having the urge to make comparisons,' then refocus your attention back into the room. We could see what happens. (Therapist suggests alternative behaviour that can be done as homework practice, and encourages the client to be interested in the outcome.)

This time the therapist has chosen to shape Joan's awareness of how quickly she moved into social comparisons when experiencing anxiety. This might be very useful if her problems are to do with low self-esteem or social anxiety.

These two extracts demonstrate the real art of taking feedback; the therapist has a constant eye on the aspect of the practice that will produce the highest take-home value for the client. She uses the brief window of opportunity after each exercise to guide the client's awareness strategically. She moves gently back and forth from a micro-analysis of the practice to a broader view of the client's everyday life, a skill that can be described as shifting focus between the forest and the trees.

Awareness involves the ability to take a 'metacognitive' position, stepping back from the content of our mind, and noticing the process it is going through, noticing how it wanders, fixates, repeats itself, and all outside of our volition. It is the uninvited actions of the mind that cause us the most problems, so from time to time as teachers we may ask, "did you invite your mind to do that?" For example, if Joan had reported, "I started to think, I'm no good at this mindfulness stuff" Tina might have asked, "Did you *invite* your mind to judge you? Did you say to yourself, 'I think now would be a great time to assess just how well I'm doing at mindfulness today'?" To which Joan is most likely to answer, "No."

During mindfulness feedback, look out for opportunities to highlight these automatic responses.

There are two common responses that crop up in mindfulness feedback that can unsettle a new teacher. One is if the client says, "I struggled with that practice." Usually, the best response to this is to ask, "How did 'struggle' show up? Did it come in the form of a thought? Or a sensation? Or an urge? How did struggle make itself known to you?" Once the client has unhooked from the label of 'struggle' you can often make good headway in how to cope with the thoughts, sensations or urges.

Another regular response is for client to say, "I just thought, I can't do this" or "I don't want to do this" or "I don't like this." Again, a simple and effective response is to ask, "When exactly did you have those thoughts, was it at the beginning, as soon as I gave the instructions? Or in the middle, after you had tried a little bit? Or at the end, when I asked you about your experience?" Questions about timing direct the client back to being mindful. Then you can ask some follow-up questions, such as, "When you had that thought, did it make doing the practice easier or harder? Did you persevere or stop? Do you ever have those thoughts outside of here?"

Acceptance of the present moment

The third component of mindfulness, turning up the impact of the current moment, can be enhanced by drawing the client's attention to the information coming through the five senses, and noting what deflects the client from accepting reality as it is being experienced.

TINA.   When you started to have urges to look round, did that get in the way of your ability to just notice the colours of the cone? (Therapist highlights consequences of attending to urges.)

JOAN.   Yes, I only seemed to see the black part after that because it was different to what I thought it should be like.

TINA.   And can you see any other colours now? (Therapist encourages additional practice of mindful awareness using the senses.)

JOAN.   Yes, there are a few different shades of brown and some grey patches.

TINA.   So, we almost have two cones competing here: your mind's version of what a cone should be like, and this actual cone in your hand. (Therapist highlights the internal obstacle that prevented the client mindfully observing the cone.)

JOAN.   But only one is real, right? I think I often do that: get all flustered about what things should be like.

TINA.   And that kind of attachment to how you'd like things to be takes you away from reality, so maybe you miss out on what's actually there. You could watch out for that: notice those attachments and refocus on the input from your senses. (Therapist labels an 'attachment' and guides the client on what to do differently.)

Unhooking from attachments to certain types of feedback

Once we have issued an invitation for a client to share their feedback it is important to remember that when they give their response, they are doing the required task – sharing their observations. We need to unhook from any attachment to what the observations 'should' be. The experienced mindfulness teacher will treat all feedback as 'grist to the mill.'

Alan is taking some feedback after a group mindfulness task in which clients listened to some music mindfully. One of the clients, Paul, says, "I can't believe how much I got out of listening to this track. Usually, I only listen to music while I am driving or using my computer. I never just sit and listen like this. I could hear harmonies that I never even noticed before. It was amazing, I really enjoyed it."

Alan enquires whether Paul began evaluating his experience during the exercise or afterwards. He highlights that engaging in evaluation at the same time as listening might momentarily deflect Paul's attention away from the experience. He also asks how the pleasure manifested itself, guiding Paul to pay attention to these sensations so that he can notice them at other times. He asks whether Paul can make time for some mindful listening at other times during the week, and what might get in the way. Paul says, "I'll think that I should be working." Alan encourages him to notice the thought without acting on it and then refocus on the music.

Now Alan turns to the group and asks, "Did anyone have a different experience?" Corinne says, "Yeah, I hate that type of music so I got really bored. I stopped listening and started making a shopping list in my head."

Alan keeps the same interested tone and facial expression with Corinne as he did with Paul. He enquires whether she had a thought, such as 'this is boring' or if some kind of physical sensation came first. He elicits a micro-chain of events between the thought and abandoning the task to think about something else. He directs Corinne to notice whether sensations such as irritation in her body went away when she distracted herself.

Finally, he asks Corinne if the thought 'this is boring' ever resulted in her giving up on other tasks. She says, "Yeah, I suppose so. I have some passport forms to fill in, but it's so boring I keep putting it off." Alan wonders if she might be willing to just notice the thought 'this is boring' and to practise returning her mind to the forms, even in the presence of the uncomfortable sensations.

In this example Alan uses the same principles in responding to Paul's feedback as he does to Corinne's. In each case he is looking for aspects of the practice that might enhance the client's skill, watching for opportunities to strengthen insight and encourage new behaviour. A less experienced therapist might assume that Paul's more positive experience is desirable and Corinne's is not. In fact, both sets of comments give equal opportunity for teaching mindfulness skills. There is even an argument that a practice that elicits some kind of discomfort can be more valuable than one that is routinely pleasant. This is because most clients in therapy are seeking some relief from their uncomfortable internal experiences. For this reason, therapists should think carefully before dropping certain exercises from their mindfulness repertoire just because clients dislike them, as illustrated in the next example.

Jake and Allie run a mindfulness group for adolescents. They find that their clients really enjoy the active participation exercises, such as throwing balloons, blowing bubbles or playing Jenga mindfully. Whenever the facilitators suggest a less active practice the group members express disapproval, either verbally, through their body language or in their facial expressions. Over time Jake and Allie find themselves working harder and harder to invent more creative or interesting exercises. The clients have shaped the facilitators' behaviour by using aversive consequences. As a result, they have lots of fun in the sessions but do not learn from quieter practices.

Jake sums up the dilemma: "Our clients frequently get into trouble at college for not focusing on the lesson. Often, they are distracted by worry thoughts stemming from interpersonal conflicts at home or with friends. They find it hard to turn their minds away from such intense internal stimulation in order to focus on schoolwork."

Together Jake and Allie decide to ask the adolescents to come up with some exercises that they would consider 'boring' for them all to practise on. They agree as a group to vary between the active and quiet exercises in order to get some practice at 'urge surfing' – continuing what they are doing even in the presence of the urge to quit. They construct a hierarchy of exercises from most to least boring and give a prize for the one getting the most votes at the end of the month. They encourage feedback after each exercise and it is quickly noted by the clients that what one person finds boring is not the same for everyone else.

The set of exercises give Jake and Allie some rich teaching points about the thought 'it's boring.'

- It can be an assumption (when the activity turns out to be fun after all).
- It can also be a judgement (it's boring and that's a very, very bad thing).
- It can also be just a thought passing through our mind.
- It can act as a trigger or 'permission-giving thought' to allow our mind to wander to other topics.
- It can stop people even starting an activity if they predict it will bore them.

Here are some of the 'boring' practices the adolescents came up with:

- Sit still and stare at the wall without moving.
- Sip a glass of water very slowly.
- Count to ten slowly, then count backwards from ten to one, then start again.
- Watch the 'windows circle shining GIF' (Google it).

Letting go of ego

Therapists can occasionally get caught up in their own judgements about their performance, especially in the face of what might be experienced as critical feedback. This is an opportunity for the mindfulness teacher to practise the skill themselves.

Eric has just led a mindfulness exercise.

CERYS. We did this last week with Polly and she led it much better than you.

ERIC. And did you make that evaluation right at the start? Or at the end? Or only when I asked what happened? (Therapist gets straight into encouraging curiosity about the experience.)

CERYS As soon as you started doing the body scan, I thought that Polly went a lot quicker.

ERIC. And did that 'comparison' thought take you away from my instructions? (Therapist labels comparisons and draws the client's attention to consequences.)

CERYS. Not really, I did what you said but then I kept on thinking that you were so slow.

ERIC. So, the comparison thought kept returning. Did it get stronger or more frequent as time went on? (Therapist highlights the repetitive nature of the thought and encourages further curiosity.)

CERYS. No, it kind of went away. I suppose I got used to the pace.

ERIC. So as the pace became more familiar you got less attached to how it was last week? (Therapist highlights the role of familiarity and attachment in this experience.)

CERYS. Maybe.

ERIC. What do you think you did that contributed to the thought becoming less intense? (Therapist doesn't push the learning point, but focuses the client on internal actions that might have been effective.)

CERYS. I just did what you were telling us to do.

ERIC. That's a very mindful observation. Throwing yourself into the task in this moment reduced the impact of those comparisons. That might be helpful to know if ever your mind gets stuck in comparing the present unfavourably with the past. I think we all find our minds

> do that from time to time. (Therapist points out mindful behaviour, reiterates the consequences, normalises the phenomenon and describes how the learning can help in the client's everyday life.)

In this example Eric does not get defensive about the differences in the way he and Polly lead the body scan; instead, he uses the comments to highlight a new learning point for the client. He is also modelling acceptance by not trying to change the client's mind about the relative merits of each therapist's natural style.

"But what's the point, teacher?"

When clients have not been referred specifically to learn how to be mindful the orientation process can be ongoing. A typical response with new clients might be for them to question the value of the practice. For example, a number of therapists have guided a client through being mindful of eating a raisin, only to be asked at the end of the practice, "so, what?" At this juncture the therapist may well experience either frustration or self-doubt. Having a range of responses available can reduce the likelihood that the therapist will slip into unmindful thoughts.

- The therapist can relate the practice of mindfulness to the client's goals for therapy. For example: "Have you ever had a situation where something went wrong at work and then you just couldn't get it out of your head all night? Would it have been helpful if you could have had the skill to unhook from those thoughts?"
- The therapist can give a personal example of using mindfulness. For example: "I've found this skill really useful when I want to have another coffee before bedtime but I know it will

keep me awake. I realise that I can just observe that urge and it will fade. I don't have to either drink coffee or eat chocolate to get rid of it."

- The therapist can tell a story or use a metaphor. "Once upon a time there was a man who lived in a block of flats. Every morning he checked the free newspaper that came through his door to see what the weather would be like. Each day he either took his umbrella or his scarf or wore no coat, depending on the printed forecast. Invariably he was caught out. One day he grumbled about it to his neighbour. 'Sorry,' said his friend, 'I always get to that paper first, then I push it through your door the next day, when I've read it.' Sometimes our minds are like this: they feed us yesterday's news, but we react to it as though it's fact."

- The therapist can take a metacognitive position. For example: "It can be really hard to stick with something when we notice that 'what's the point?' thought. Sometimes it helps us find an answer, and at other times it just gets in the way of us doing something. What happens for you when you get that thought?"

There are many possible responses and the role of the therapist is to stay light and easy in manner, and to avoid judging the client for what is a very understandable question. Another problem for the therapist can be when the client goes one step further than asking "what's the point?" and defends or justifies an unmindful stance.

> DEAN. It's no good trying to focus on my breath, I've got a heap of worries that I really need to be thinking about. I could lose the house the way things are going.
> RUTH. That sounds like a serious problem. Does it seem as though hanging onto your worry thoughts is a way of solving it?

DEAN.   Or at least trying to solve it, yeah.

RUTH.   (Thoughtfully.) OK, I see. Whenever you have thoughts about losing the house do you immediately go into some kind of action that could perhaps save the house, like planning what you could do?

DEAN.   No, because I know what I have to do. I'm waiting to hear from the bank, and about my job.

RUTH.   So at least some of the time the thoughts don't actually lead to any immediate progress on the house issue?

DEAN.   Er, no, not really.

RUTH.   And tell me, on the occasions when they are not helping you with the house issue, are they still helpful in some way? (Pause) Or do they sometimes get in the way of your daily routines?

DEAN.   If you mean, 'Do they wind me up?' Yes, they do. Then I get in a fight with my girlfriend. But it seems wrong to just let them go.

RUTH.   You know what, our minds naturally go over things to try and solve problems, but they're not so good at turning this off when you have a plan and are waiting for more information to come through. I'm thinking that mindfulness might be a useful skill so you can turn your mind from the 'house' thoughts at certain times, and turn it back when you need to. We can keep practising the skill and then you can try it out in those different situations and see how it goes. You've got so much on your plate right now and I'm definitely not here to make your life worse, so if you have the skill and it's not useful, you can just not use it. But if it *does* help it sounds like you could really do with that bit of respite.

The role of the therapist is to position themselves on the side of the client. The most vociferous dissent can be turned around this way.

BRUNO. I'm done with this rubbish. My life is falling apart and you're getting me to hold a shell? That's your therapy, is it? I am wasting my time here.

VAL. Oh no, Bruno, it sounds like that was three minutes of misery, for you. Were those thoughts about your life falling apart just going through your mind all the time?

BRUNO. (Rolls his eyes.) Yes, because it IS falling apart! You don't seem to get that.

VAL. I can see this is how it looks, and that's my fault, because I don't think I have explained it well enough. I think that your mind is torturing you, day and night, and that just isn't fair to you. You're exhausted. And I just want to be able to help you get some control back.

BRUNO. How is looking at a shell getting me any control back?

VAL. It doesn't have to be a shell, and in your shoes, I'd be thinking the same thing. The shell doesn't matter, I just want to help you in any given moment be able to turn off the tap of those misery-making thoughts, and focus on something else, ANYTHING else. We're practicing on the shell, but eventually I want YOU to be able to choose. I want YOU to have the power to divert your attention where YOU want it to go. And if you could, if I could help you with that, so that you never again have to be kept awake all night with thoughts you don't want, that you can't even do anything about right then, would you be interested?

BRUNO. (Sags in the chair.) Of course I would. I just don't believe it can happen like this.

> VAL. That makes complete sense. Your mind is telling you it can't happen. Do you want to get some power over that?
>
> BRUNO. (Sits back.) Man, this is hard.
>
> VAL. It IS hard, and it takes practice. You could easily have stormed out, and you didn't. Well done for that. Remember we're 100% on your side. Stay with it Bruno, we're willing you on.

In a group, this kind of exchange often results in other group members offering support to the person who is struggling.

In this chapter we have shown how the therapist can use the feedback period after each exercise to shape the skill. We have also addressed some common responses that can challenge the therapist.

Key tasks

- Ask what the client noticed during the practice.
- Highlight where the client was mindful.
- Put labels on internal experiences: types of thoughts, sensations, emotions, urges.
- Pull as much experience as possible into the client's awareness.
- Keep to one or two learning points per feedback.
- Link in-session practice to day-to-day life.
- Suggest what the client can do differently.

Stylistic factors

- Adopt a light, interested tone.
- Vary the viewpoint 'between the forest and the trees.'
- Do not judge the client for giving information about their experience.
- Let go of defensiveness and ego.
- Treat both positively and negatively phrased feedback in an identical manner.
- Always look for the teaching point.
- Position yourself on the client's side.
- Avoid being shaped by the client into responding in one particular way.

Mindfulness
of thoughts

Being mindful of thoughts is a key skill and, in our experience, one where clients often struggle. We can be so caught up in our thoughts that it can be hard to see ourselves and our thoughts as separate. One of the main challenges in teaching mindfulness skills is to help clients take a step back and, with kindly curiosity, recognise their thoughts as transient mental events.

As we have said in Chapter 4, the art of teaching mindfulness is in taking feedback after a practice. If we are focusing on thoughts, we may ask specific questions such as "Did you notice that thought?" "When did it come?" and "What happened then?" By modelling openness and curiosity, we encourage the client to change their relationship with their thoughts by noticing, with compassion, that they come and go. They may also begin to notice that a thought can lead to an emotion, a sensation or an urge. For example, the thought 'I have forgotten my keys' may be followed by a feeling of anxiety and the urge to check our pockets.

Clients will often say, "But that's not a thought; it's a fact." Helping people to unhook from whether a thought is factual or not can be quite tricky. Sometimes all that is needed is a gentle reminder, such as when a client says, "I'm going to get sacked for being late so often." It might be easy for them to see that this

DOI: 10.4324/9781003386117-5

is an assumption. But for some thoughts the client will use the expression "it actually *feels* like a fact." When a thought is associated with high emotion it can often make it harder to distance yourself from it and notice it's a thought. Here is a common example.

Janet was very anxious in social situations and would often have the thought 'I'm worthless.' The thought seemed so true to her that she found it hard to use the mindfulness skills she was learning and notice it as a thought, allowing it to come and go. In their session, her therapist pointed out that she could have the thought 'I'm worthless' or have the thought 'I'm a purple cat.' Both are thoughts. Having the thought makes her no more a purple cat than it makes her worthless. The humorous image helped Janet to take a step back, take a more curious stance and start to label 'I'm worthless' as a thought.

Caught up in content

The main problem for all of us in detaching from our thoughts is the speed at which we get pulled into the subject matter without *consciously* deciding to do so. The following extract is taken from a teaching session where the therapist explains this concept to a small group of clients, starting with a personal example.

I was at work and had the thought 'I have run out of milk.' In a flash I was thinking 'If I leave work promptly and take a detour, I can pop into the corner shop and pick up some milk and still be back in time to meet the kids from school.' I had had the thought and attached to the content without even realising it.

This fast-processing can, of course, be very helpful. It can also cause problems when the content of the thought leads us to have painful emotional responses or to behave in ways we don't want to. Now let's imagine the scenario again, with a different set of thoughts.

> I was at work and had the thought 'I'm so stupid; I've run out of milk.' In a flash I was thinking 'Why do I always do this? I never think ahead and I'm always forgetting things. Now I will be late and I won't be there when the children get home from school. How can I be such an idiot?' I started to think about all the other times I've messed up and felt really sad.

In the second scenario we can see that instead of helping us solve our problem of having no milk, our rapid train of thought took us down a very different route. When we are being mindful, we do not assume that the first scenario is good, and the second is bad. Instead, we learn the skill of 'stepping back.'

The therapist skilfully chose a second scenario that would resonate with her clients, many of whom suffered from low self-esteem. Using the therapist's example as a guide, the clients were able to identify recurrent thoughts that take them down well-worn paths and away from the reality of the situation.

Choosing whether to act on our thoughts

In her mindfulness DVD, *This One Moment: Skills for Everyday Mindfulness*, Marsha Linehan (1995) describes how early on in mindfulness training she would practise being mindful of her breath. During the practice she would have the urge to quit and then simply stop. It was a long time before she realised she could have the urge to quit and just notice it *without acting on it*. As mindfulness teachers, we are often helping clients to become aware of their thoughts so that they can make a conscious choice either to follow them or not. Here are two teaching examples, one from a client perspective, and another told as a personal anecdote.

Client perspective

Beth had been bullied at school. As she grew up, she developed a habit of always doing things for others, so that she would fit in. Whenever someone asked her to do something for them Beth would think they would only like her if she agreed. She would go to great lengths even though this often led her to feel resentful and to think she was being used. By learning mindfulness Beth recognised that she was getting caught up in the content of her thought 'they'll only like me if I do it for them' and following this automatically. She learned to become aware of her thoughts and notice the urge to do things for others without acting on it. Eventually she found the urge would pass and she could weigh up whether she really wanted to help out or not. She was surprised when some people liked her despite her sometimes saying no to them.

Personal anecdote

I had some feedback from a colleague at work the other day commenting negatively on the approach I had taken. I had the urge to jump in and defend myself but I did not act on it. Rather I told my colleague I would think about his comments and get back to him. On reflection there were some comments I agreed with and some I didn't. I was able to talk to my colleague in a much more balanced way for having been mindful and taking the time to decide whether to act on my thoughts or not.

Using personal examples

There are a number of reasons to use personal examples in teaching mindfulness, but probably the most powerful is that clients really like it. They tell us that it brings the teaching to life. It also demonstrates that we are no different from our clients; we need to use the skills as much as they do. Finally, it inspires confidence in the techniques as we can demonstrate using them in a variety of circumstances. For the mindfulness teacher, every journey, event or catastrophe is an opportunity to gather new material, although there are also some important factors to consider.

- Will I be contravening any guidelines in my working environment if I choose to share these details? For example, in some forensic settings it is considered inappropriate to give out any personal information.
- Is the story one that involves a 'live' issue for me? If the example involves current emotions, now might not be the time to share.
- Does the story actually demonstrate the teaching point that I am working on during this session? If in doubt ask a colleague.
- Will it resonate with the client's circumstances?

- Do I feel comfortable with this example? Does this story fit my usual way of working? A 'forced' style is rarely effective. The skilled mindfulness teacher tries to develop a very natural manner, slipping easily between personal stories and clinical examples.

Context of the thought

Another teaching point is that the context of the thought will have an impact on the experience.

Let's think of two examples:

In the first you have been playing football with your team. The game didn't go well for you. You are upset because you failed to pass to a team member which resulted in the opposition scoring a goal. Then, near the end of the game, you were offside and the free kick led to the opposing team scoring the second, winning, goal. Later you are walking out of the changing room when you see a team member, who turns and hurries away saying: "I can't stop now."

What are your thoughts likely to be? How will they impact on you?

In the second example, you have been playing football with your team. The game went really well for you. You are really happy because you passed to a team member which resulted in them scoring a goal. Then, near the end of the game, you took a free kick which led to your team scoring the second, winning, goal. Later you are walking out of the changing room when you see a team member, who turns and hurries away saying: "I can't stop now."

What are your thoughts likely to be? How will they impact on you? Is there any difference to the first example?

Examples like this can be fun ways of helping clients to see that context matters and being mindful of the context can help to unhook from thoughts when they are painful and having a negative impact on us. Another way can be the use of metaphors.

Use of metaphors

Once clients have identified their internal phenomenon as a thought, they need to acquire the skill of unhooking from it. We usually refer to this skill as 'letting go of thoughts without attaching to content.' Sometimes just labelling the thought will be enough.

Claire's husband was late home from work. She began to think about all the potential accidents that might have befallen him. Her anxiety was slowly mounting. Then she remembered her mindfulness teaching and was able to say, 'I am having worry thoughts.' Immediately she felt as though she had taken her hand off a hot plate. The process of labelling the thoughts enabled her to let them go. As each thought returned, she told herself, 'That's another worry thought.'

Some thoughts can be much harder to release. Clients may make the mistake of trying to battle with the thoughts, leading to a rebound effect. This is when the use of metaphors can be enormously effective. One of our favourites is a visual metaphor.

Thoughts that are really hard to unhook from are like 'sticky' thoughts. The harder you push away the more they stick around. What happens when we 'push' something? (The therapist makes a pushing motion with her hand.) What we get is the sensation of the thought 'pushing back.'

Let's see what happens if we try to loosen our grip on the thought instead. (The therapist holds a tissue in her fingers and then gently opens them, allowing the tissue to fall to the ground.)

But what if we have been doing some kind of craft work and our hands have got some glue on them? We might open our hand but the tissue doesn't immediately fall. We have to resist the urge to wrestle with it, getting more and more covered in glue. Instead, we need to keep repeating the same action until it eventually slides from our open hand.

Metaphors that have a special meaning for your client can be particularly powerful. For instance, a client who loved to drive used to allow thoughts to come and go by imagining putting the thought in a car and watching it drive away. Transportation or motion metaphors are always popular as they convey the concept of 'letting go' through the image of movement.

Here is a list of metaphors that we have come across that illustrate the 'transient' nature of thoughts.

- Thoughts can be like buses, sometimes hardly any arrive and sometimes they come all together.
- We can notice each of our thoughts like clouds floating in the sky.
- Thoughts can be like birds flying overhead. We don't need to catch them; they will just fly on.

- Some thoughts can be easy to let go, like a tissue floating from your hand, others can be much harder, like the tissue stuck to your hand with glue after crafting activity.

- Standing back from our thoughts can be like watching a train as it goes through the station. Our task is to stay on the platform and watch as it passes by.

- Watching our thoughts can be like scrolling through our email inbox: we can pass over some of the emails, noticing that they are there without having to open each one.

- Noticing our thoughts can be like standing on the side of a stream, watching the leaves as they float past, with each leaf carrying a thought.

- Thoughts come and go like food on a sushi belt.

If your clients like a metaphor, you can expand on it with them. The buses metaphor can be extended so your client imagines putting the thought on the front of the bus. Then asking themselves: 'I can get on that bus but I know where it takes me. Or I can stay at the bus stop and watch it go by.' This can be particularly helpful with difficult or painful thoughts.

Jabari was teaching mindfulness of thoughts in a group session.

JABARI. Being mindful is like watching our thoughts go by like leaves on a stream, while we stand on the bank. Sometimes you're on the edge of the stream watching them go by and sometimes they are rushing past and the stream is like a torrent and you fall in.

(Jabari makes a jumping action to show falling into the stream. His speech speeds up and he waves his arms as if trying to move leaves away.)

> You get caught up in the leaves and they are tangled all around you. You try to get free from them but the leaves keep coming and… (speech slowing) your task is to get back on the bank (steps to one side) and watch the leaves go by.
>
> Does it ever feel like sometimes you are caught up in the leaves and the stream is a raging torrent?

Sometimes a metaphor enables us to make more than one point. Here is another of our favourites.

> Sushi belt: Sometimes our thoughts seem to come round and round again, like the food passing by on a sushi belt. Some things look really tempting and we want to take them off, others look strange and we want to push them away, but the task is just to notice them as they pass by. Of course, it can be hard to let certain things go by. We may have a thought like 'I'm stupid,' and as it comes in front of us, we are really tempted to engage with it. But beware! Every time we devour that thought you can guarantee that someone in the kitchen is shouting, "Hey, those 'I'm stupid' thoughts are going really well. Let's get a few more of those on the sushi belt."

Distinguishing between mindfulness and metaphor

If we are evoking an image such as 'putting your thoughts on a cloud and watching it float away,' the teacher needs to be clear that this is a metaphor and not a mindfulness of clouds exercise. The distinguishing feature is that, if we were being mindful of clouds, we would go outside and look up at real clouds, watching them actually float by.

It is possible to do a visualisation exercise mindfully, i.e., with your full attention and interest, but the teacher has to take care to avoid confusing the client. It is wise to clearly distinguish between metaphor, guided imagery and mindfulness.

Myths about mindfulness

Dispelling myths clients may have about mindfulness is important. Mindfulness of your thoughts is not about emptying your mind or being in a trance. Nor is it about being happy all the time or only having positive thoughts. Rather it is noticing your thoughts *as thoughts*. For example, if I am holding a red pen, I can have the thought, 'this pen is red,' or I can have the thought 'this pen is blue.' One is accurate, the other is not, but either way, both were simply 'thoughts about the pen.' Whatever the content, thoughts are passing mental events that come and go. In mindfulness we are not judging thoughts as good or bad, true or false, we are just noticing them with kindly interest and curiosity. It can help to say to your clients, "If you get caught up in the content and find yourself going down a rabbit warren of thoughts, don't tell yourself off or get down on yourself, try saying to yourself: 'thoughts,' take a mental step back and notice the next thought that comes up."

Practising being mindful of thoughts

Before we begin our practical exercises, we may draw the client's attention to some key points:

- Thoughts can come as words or images.
- There are no right or wrong thoughts.

- We are not attempting to challenge or change our thoughts, just to notice them.
- Opening our posture (e.g., shoulders back and lowered) can help us to open our mind.

In one exercise we may simply ask clients to be aware of the thoughts that pass through their mind for a particular period of time, perhaps two minutes. We keep the practices very short as many people find being mindful of thoughts particularly challenging. We would give the instruction that if they get caught up in the content of a thought, to notice and gently bring their mind back to the next thought. Sometimes the teacher will give the instruction to say to yourself: "I'm noticing the thought…" A demonstration is often helpful, speaking aloud the observations so that the client can understand what is required.

> I am noticing the thought, 'You are watching me.' I am noticing the thought, 'This is quite hard to do.' I am noticing the thought, 'I don't think I am doing this right.' I am noticing the thought, 'I should keep still.' I am noticing the image of my woollen gloves. I am noticing the thought, 'That was strange to think about my gloves.'

Another practice would be to notice the thoughts as before but to give them a factual label: for example, a thought about the other person, a thought about the task, a worry thought and so on. In each case the client is learning to take a metacognitive position, i.e., one step back from the content of their thoughts.

After leading a practice like this it is not uncommon for a client to say, "My mind was so busy and then as soon as we started it went completely blank. There wasn't a single thought." The aim would be to explore their experience: "Did you have the thought 'My mind has gone completely blank' at the time or is it looking back on it now that you think that?" Often people will have had this very thought during the exercise without recognising that it *is* a thought. However, it is also possible that they may indeed have had no thoughts and then the aim is to explore in a kindly and interested way the experience of having a few moments without thoughts.

What am I if I am not my thoughts?

Having explained that our thoughts are not facts, and that we can notice them without attaching to them, we may encounter some searching questions from clients about the nature of the self. One client asked, "Who is it that is stepping back from my thoughts?" Our recommendation is to treat these questions in a light and easy manner. Clients sometimes appreciate the analogy of using the term 'my leg,' which acknowledges that the leg is part of us, but not the whole. Just as we can acknowledge an existence that might *not* include our leg, we can also acknowledge an existence that might *not* include these particular thoughts.

Thoughts leading to emotions

A client may feedback that the thought they were having gave them an emotional reaction. For example, they may have noticed feeling sad and wanting to cry during the practice. As a mindfulness teacher it is important not to be put off by the client becoming upset in the practice, rather we should help them notice the process by which that happened. By gentle interest in their experience the client may realise, for example, that they had a thought about a recent argument with a friend, felt sad and noticed tears pricking the back of their eyes. By accepting this we are modelling that neither our thoughts nor our physical experiences are to be feared, held onto or rejected. We are encouraging clients to notice links between thoughts, bodily sensations and emotions.

This is one of the areas that therapists find the most challenging. They will often become attached to the idea that mindfulness should be a 'positive' or pleasant experience. They can find themselves making a judgement that if the client experiences a painful emotion the therapist has 'failed' or the exercise has been unsuccessful. In fact, the opposite is often closer to the truth. Clients often go to great lengths to avoid certain thoughts or emotions, causing problems in their everyday life. Learning to accept both the thought and emotion without fear can be hugely liberating.

Sometimes therapists will be uncomfortable if they are dealing with clients who engage in dangerous acts to get rid of painful emotions, for example if clients self-harm or assault others. Mindfulness, like any other intervention, should always be conducted with attention to risk management procedures, and with reference to each client's personal risk profile. Our advice is not to seek out evocative practices in the early stages, but where an emotion naturally occurs as a result of the practice, to model observing and accepting the accompanying sensations. Finally, conduct an assessment before the client leaves the session to ensure they are refocused on the present and not still caught up in the emotion. If this is difficult for them, instructing the client in mindfully using grounding strategies can be very helpful such as noticing the floor under our feet and the feel of the chair we are sitting on, or observing five things we can see, taste, touch, smell and hear in the present moment.

Categories of thoughts

Clients will often say that they find giving thoughts factual labels is very useful in helping them to take a step back and notice them as thoughts. By repeating this exercise, they may find that there are particular categories of thoughts that they tend to have in certain situations. The mindfulness teacher will help to identify categories specific to the client and also 'generic' categories that other clients have found helpful. Clients frequently describe finding it very validating that others engage in the same type of thinking. Some categories that clients often find useful are:

- worry thoughts
- sticky thoughts
- catastrophising or 'the worst thing' thoughts
- self-critical thoughts
- camouflaged or hidden thoughts, i.e., thoughts that are hard to detect, e.g., 'I can't do this' or 'this will never help' – they often come with high emotion that can make them hard to recognise as thoughts
- storytelling thoughts
- associations
- interpretations
- judgements.

A useful practice can be for the client to mindfully write down the top five or ten categories or patterns of thoughts or images that they find particularly challenging. Writing them down can help give space to identify them as thoughts, notice them when they crop up and recognise the impact they have on the experience. The last three categories – associations, interpretations and judgements – will be discussed in more detail.

Mindfulness of associations

When highlighting associations to clients it is important to explain why it could be useful to them to notice that their mind has made an association and that this is a natural thing that minds do.

Jodie was an experienced mindfulness therapist leading a mindfulness practice in group. She gave each client a piece of lavender and guided them to experience the lavender with all their five senses.

In the feedback Fay said, "I started to smell the lavender and it reminded me of being back in my grandmother's house, which always smelled of lavender. It reminded me of all the happy times I had there." Jodie asked if Fay noticed that this was an association. When Fay said she did, Jodie asked whether, when she had noticed this, she had brought her mind back to experiencing the lavender in the present. Fay replied, "I noticed but those were such happy times I decided to stay with it."

Jodie acknowledged the desire to stay with the nice memories but asked if Fay would be willing to try noticing the association and bringing her mind back to the lavender in the present. Jodie gently reminded Fay that whilst on this occasion the association was pleasant, sometimes associations are painful. By practising returning her mind from a pleasant association there is more chance that Fay will have developed the skill well enough to use with a painful one.

In teaching mindfulness, we are helping clients to see that there are different ways of responding so that they have choices. It is important to validate the desire to stay with pleasant associations and also to ask if they ever found their mind going onto painful associations. A pleasant association will be a 'sticky' thought in the same way that a distressing association is 'sticky,' so it provides an excellent practise opportunity. We have found that clients are often very willing to do this – although it is hard – as they recognise how helpful this skill could be to them in so many different situations.

John had suffered from depression for many years. Through attending therapy, he had started to increase his activities and go to an art class that he really enjoyed. He went with his good friend Bob, every week. When Bob moved to a different part of the country John stopped going to the art class and became more depressed. When he thought of attending the class, he remembered how much he missed his friend and felt sad. He would think of all the times people had left him in the past, and the pain of all these losses would feel overwhelming. He stayed away despite other class members phoning and encouraging him to come.

Using mindfulness John recognised how the thought of art class triggered associations: not only with the loss of Bob but with many past losses and the sadness that they evoked. He realised this pattern kept him trapped in a cycle of avoidance and sadness that felt overwhelming. With practise he was able to notice where his mind had gone to, label it as an association and gently bring himself back to the present. With the help of his therapist, he learned to be aware of the sadness he felt for missing his friend without the associations of all his past losses. He was then able to participate in the class once again, remembering to stay in the present moment of each session.

Mindfulness of interpretations

When highlighting interpretations, it can be helpful to make the teaching point that an interpretation is the meaning which we put onto an event. Different interpretations will elicit different emotional reactions.

Helen and her coach were discussing being mindful of interpretations. Jo, the therapist, described how she had sneezed when the group were being mindful of sound. She had then had the thought, 'I have disturbed everyone' and noticed the emotion of guilt. She then mindfully labelled the thought as an interpretation and noticed the guilt went down.

Helen told Jo about using her mindfulness skills whilst out shopping. She had noticed the thought 'they are doing this to wind me up' when a shop assistant was being very slow taking her money. She mindfully noticed the interpretation and was able to restate this factually to herself, 'I notice I am becoming tense in my muscles whilst I am waiting for my change.' She noticed the anxiety came down almost immediately.

Mindfulness of judgements

An important category of thoughts that can cause difficulties for both clients and teachers is that of judgements. We usually start by dispelling the myth that we are saying people should never make judgements, which are of course a short-hand way of communicating. Rather, the aim is to be aware when we make judgements and be able to let them go.

When we teach mindfulness skills, we are helping people to unhook from evaluative judgements such as good/bad, right/wrong, should/shouldn't. We are teaching them to adopt a non-judgemental stance so that they have this option to use when it would be most effective.

Alec really disliked his co-worker, Jim. One morning he saw Jim approaching his desk and said to himself, 'Why is he coming over here? Up to no good, snooping round my desk to see what I'm doing, trying to get one over on me. He shouldn't even be on this floor. I bet he's messed something up and wants me to fix it.' By the time Jim got to his desk it was as much as Alec could do to snarl, "What is it, I'm really busy?"

"Oh, sorry," said Jim, "it's just that you've left your car lights on."

An important teaching point is that judgements are not just what we say but the way that we say it. Our tone of voice, facial expressions and body language will all communicate either a judgemental or non-judgemental approach. As mindfulness teachers it is important to alert clients to the *internal tone of voice* of their thoughts, to help discern whether they are judgements or not.

Learning to distinguish between preferences, opinions and judgements

Therapists often really struggle with this concept and as a result can end up teaching it incorrectly to the client. On many occasions we have heard a client say, "I really disliked that practice" only to be told by the therapist, "that's a judgement." In fact, the client is just describing her experience – she did actually dislike the practice. If a client says they liked the mindfulness practice last week better than the one today this is also their opinion or preference. We all have opinions and can even hold them very strongly. If the tone of voice, body language or facial expression implies that it is therefore *bad or wrong* of the mindfulness teacher to lead such a practice then that would be a judgement.

It can be helpful to ask "Was there a good/bad evaluation behind that? Did you think it was wrong of me to choose this practice?" If this was the case then it can be helpful to notice the judgement and let it go or encourage the client to mindfully restate it factually, e.g., "I felt anxious when we did the mindfulness of a biscuit and I didn't like that feeling."

It can help to explain that judgements are short-hand ways of saying things but they often don't tell us that much. For instance, if we said "The film was really good," it wouldn't communicate what the film was about or whether anyone else would enjoy it. A more mindful description would be to say "We really enjoyed the film because it had lots of car chases and fast action scenes that were very exciting."

The consequences of judging

Judgements often push up our emotions.

> Anya was in a railway carriage when some revellers got in after a party. She became disturbed by their noise and moved to a different carriage. "I did the right thing, just walking away," she said. "But I was fuming for the rest of the journey."

Her therapist asked: "Did you also walk away in your mind or did you spend your time in the new carriage making judgements?" Anya laughed. "Yes," she said, "I was making a lot of judgements, so it is hardly surprising that my anger didn't go down. I needed to practise my mindfulness when I got to the new carriage, noticing the urge to judge, and bringing my mind back to the current moment."

In mindfulness practice we are helping clients to develop the ability to experience people, events, themselves, objects and sensations in the moment without falling into the habit of judging the experience. If we judge something as good, we will want to hold onto it and if we judge it as bad, we will want to push it away. Mindfulness is neither. Rather it is having the experience in the moment and then moving on to the next moment. Sometimes clients will say they can understand why we might want them to unhook from judging something as bad or wrong, but ask why not make a positive judgement? The thing is that good/bad or right/wrong are two sides of the same coin. You can't have one without the other. If we judge some experiences as good then, by definition, some others must be bad.

The next trap for us to fall into is when we judge ourselves for making judgements. We need to just notice the judgement and let it go or restate it factually. If clients find they are making lots of judgements and it is hard to let them go, counting them can help.

Mary was shocked in her appraisal to receive feedback that colleagues found her difficult and confrontational in her approach. She started to learn mindfulness and became aware that she made judgements about herself and others a lot of the time. She had always seen herself as having high standards but realised that this involved her constantly evaluating herself as not good enough in all she did. She would drive herself even harder with thoughts that she should be doing better and making more effort. She realised she would often have these thoughts about others as well and get irritated that they did not live up to her expectations. When she first recognised how many judgements she was making, she thought how wrong it was of her to do this. Her mindfulness teacher reflected she was judging her judgements and suggested counting them could be helpful. Mary found this gave her the distance necessary to avoid getting caught up in judging. Over time she was able to identify judgements sooner and let them go. Mary noticed a change at work with others being more friendly and willing towards her. At her next appraisal her manager said that she seemed generally more relaxed and that colleagues had noted how she was much more approachable. Mary was really pleased.

A final teaching point on judgements is about the use of the words 'should' and 'shouldn't.' Sometimes 'should' means *in order to*. This is referred to as a 'conditional should.' For example, I should get up at eight *in order to* be at work by nine. Or I shouldn't go out tonight *in order to* ensure I revise for my exam tomorrow. Unfortunately, on many occasions we and our clients burden ourselves with unconditional 'shoulds.' We might think, 'I should be helpful to everyone' or 'I shouldn't bother people' without ever working through why we should or shouldn't do those things.

A client told me about a meeting she had with her son's teacher where she was able to use her mindfulness skills. Her son was having difficulties and she was keen to sort these out and work collaboratively with the teachers. Unfortunately, in previous meetings she had made a lot of judgements about the teachers and the school. These would increase her emotion and the meetings always ended with her becoming very angry, shouting at the staff and leaving before any plan had been agreed.

On this occasion, she was aware she wanted to be mindful, to notice judgements and let them go or restate factually what the problems were. She was mindful of the associations with her own school days and how unhappy these had been. She noticed when she started making associations and brought herself back to the present situation. She was aware when her mind went to interpretations and checked out the meaning of what people were saying. She noticed judgements that she was 'messing up,' took a mental step back and recognised kindly that this was a frequent thought for her, bringing herself back to what was actually being said. When she had the thought the teacher was 'just nasty' she restated factually and said to herself: 'I feel anxious when the teacher tells me about my son's behaviour. I worry she won't be kind to him.' She was mindful and present in the moment and, in this way, was able to stay for the meeting and contribute to the plan. This gave her a real sense of achievement and she came away thinking she had handled the situation well.

In this chapter we have highlighted the main teaching points for mindfulness of thoughts and the variety of ways in which we have helped clients and therapists to understand and practise this area of mindfulness.

Key tasks

- Recognise that thoughts are separate from ourselves.
- View thoughts as passing mental events.
- Notice when we are caught up in content and take a mental step back.
- Identify common categories of thoughts.
- Be able to recognise and let go of judgements.

Stylistic factors

- Use metaphors, particularly those most relevant to your client.
- Model curiosity and kindly interest in thoughts.
- Demonstrate through examples that mindfulness is a skill for everyone.

Bibliography

Linehan, M., 1995. *This One Moment: Skills for Everyday Mindfulness*. DVD. Directed by Behavioral Tech LLC. Guilford Press.

CHAPTER

6

Living mindfully

The ultimate aim of teaching clients to use mindfulness skills is not to turn them into effective meditators, but to help them to live each day more mindfully. This means being able to experience each moment through our senses, and being alive to the impact of whatever it is we are doing. We make the teaching point that most people can remember the impact of 'special moments' like holding a newborn baby or their first day in a new job or buying those boots they saved up for. It can seem as though the rest of our time is the in-between bit, just 'filler' between key events. Some people talk about 'me-time' as though this is a limited commodity to be squeezed in to an over-filled schedule. There is a good reason for this perception – our minds have the capacity to both create and inhabit a 'virtual reality world,' like an out-of-body experience. We tell our clients that the function of mindfulness is to help us to have more *in*-body experiences. Marsha Linehan (2015) describes 'participating' as one of the three major skills in mindfulness. In this chapter we are going to look at the factors that inhibit our ability to fully participate in the moment, and to give guidelines on how to encourage clients to increase their level of participation.

DOI: 10.4324/9781003386117-6

Orienting clients to mindful participation

Before we can engage clients in mindful participation it is helpful to get them to consider how being 'unmindful' might lessen the quality of their experience. As teachers we want to look for examples that will resonate with our particular client group. Here are some that we use to generate discussion.

Jeff is separated from his wife and sees his children, aged six and eight, every other weekend. He often takes them to the park, and although he may be watching them play on the climbing frame, he finds it really difficult to keep his mind in the present. On most occasions he has had some unpleasant exchange with his wife Michelle at the handover. "I go over and over what she just said to me, replaying the picture of her face as she was speaking the words." Sometimes during the children's shouts of enjoyment, he gets stricken with grief at the break-up of the marriage, remembering how things used to be. Then as the afternoon wears on he predicts how terrible he will feel handing the children back to their mother at the end of the visit and pictures in his mind how it will be when he leaves them. "I know that what I need to do is enjoy the time I *do* have with the children, instead of getting caught up in all these other distractions."

Ayesha has her own business and three children at senior school. Her life is a constant round of working, driving the children to various activities, helping with homework and looking after the house. She constantly multi-tasks:

grabbing lunch at her desk; using the hands-free phone while driving; asking the children about their day as she prepares the evening meal. She feels as though she never gives anything her undivided attention as she juggles competing demands on her time. She recently had to visit the GP and found herself working on her notepad computer in the waiting room. She says, "Half the time I am so busy I don't even know where I am." Ayesha worries that she will never get to the end of her to-do list and start to reap the benefits of all her hard work, and that she is somehow missing something as her life rushes past her in a blur of obligations.

Becky told her mindfulness teacher how she had received a call from her friend one evening, who said, "A group of us from uni were sitting in the coffee shop and you walked past. We were banging on the window and calling out but you were in a complete daze, one earpiece in, listening to your music. By the time we made our way to the entrance you'd gone, we even called your phone but you didn't answer." Becky was disappointed as her friend recounted the amusing stories from the reunion. She wondered how many other things she missed in the same way. "The thing is," said Becky, "I wasn't even really listening to the music. Sometimes I walk along in the same daze without my earphones."

After introducing each example, the therapist can ask, "Do you recognise any of this? Has this ever happened to you? Can you think of an example of a time when you were unmindful when it would have been more effective to just be in the experience?"

The most common argument given by clients is that it is essential to multi-task, as in the case of Ayesha; if she did not do her computing in the GP waiting room, then when would it get done? And what is the point of participating in 'being in the waiting room' anyway? It is just dead time. The art of teaching here is not to disagree with the clients, but to guide the discussion back to the idea of effectiveness. What do we think was the quality of the computer work done whilst waiting to see the doctor? What do we think was the mood-state of Ayesha as she snatched this time to write? How do we think this might have affected her consultation with the GP? Do we think she was subsequently more likely or less likely to recall all her symptoms or ask relevant questions?

The mindfulness teacher needs to be able to validate the difficulty of remaining in the present moment. Sometimes the therapist will set this simple homework task.

When you leave this building see how long you can manage to hold your attention on what you are experiencing on the journey. Notice any sights, sounds, smells, sensations.

Some clients report back that they had already 'lost hold of their mind' before they had even heard the click of the door closing behind them.

The time-travelling mind

The main teaching point here is that the mind has the capacity to reach forward in time to anticipate what is to come or backwards to remember what's gone. Sadly, if we do not become more aware of this process, we end up missing out on a huge proportion of our experiences.

The use of metaphor can help to explain this idea. First, set up a mindfulness practice such as the breathing exercise that we described in Chapter 3. Then ask:

When your mind left 'present island,' where did it travel to?

- The island of past memories?
- The island of future plans and predictions?
- The island of the fantasy past (if only X had happened instead of Y; if only I had done this instead of that)?
- The island of future catastrophe?

We need to notice that all these islands are in a different time zone; when we hang out there, we leave the present moment.

This metaphor prompted one of our clients to remark that whenever he had a holiday planned, he would spend all his time thinking about what he would do when he got there, and when he got there, he would spend all his time thinking about what he would do when he got back, so he was never actually *in* the experience of being on holiday.

Sometimes clients object that if they are caught up in a memory or association of the past, and they unhook from it to bring their attention to the present moment, then this is somehow invalidating their trauma or their suffering. It is vital for the therapist to clarify that this is a skill, designed to give the power back to them to decide where they put their attention. If they practise this skill, they can find that they are still able to access everything that happened to them – but at a time of their own choosing.

Participating in the present moment: How close can you get?

As therapists or mindfulness teachers we do not often get a chance to be with our clients in their day-to-day life outside of the therapy room. When they come to us for therapy there are a number of reminders to be mindful. The sight of the teacher can act as a cue, as does the layout of the room, the presence of other participants, the posture we assume, the sound of the bell if one is used. This is not the case outside and so we need to use some of the therapy time to spark up a degree of curiosity in the client: how mindful are they when they get home?

Exercise: Discuss what the difference might be in our experience of a football match in each of the following situations:

1   reading a newspaper article about a match that is due to be played next week
2   hearing your friend describe a football match he went to
3   listening to a match live on the radio
4   watching the match live on TV
5   being in the crowd at the game
6   playing in the match.

At each level the client is given two experiences to compare – starting with 1 and 2, then 2 and 3, and so on. The therapist elicits some key observations: which games have actually been played, which are in real time, which are being experienced through an interpreter (the friend, the radio reporter, the camera-man). The teacher then puts these questions to the client.

- How much do you feel that in your everyday life you are 'in contact' with your own moment-by-moment experiences?

- How much are you affected by the interpretations of your mind?

- How much is your mind giving a running commentary on every task you undertake?

- How much do you mistake this commentary for the main event?

After one such discussion a client told us, "I spend most of my life listening to a commentary by someone who never even went to the match, and doesn't like football!"

This exercise can be followed up by a participation practice in which clients are given a task to do and asked to just throw themselves in, trying not to attend to the 'running commentary' of their mind. Here are some examples of participation exercises (with thanks to the many mindfulness teachers and trainers who have taught them to us).

- Mirroring: in twos face each other. One person is the leader and makes movements that the other person copies as though they are the reflection in a mirror.

- Copying and adding movements: this is a group activity where people stand in a circle facing inwards. The first person makes a move like tapping the top of his head; the second person repeats this movement and adds a second, like bending his knees; the third person must both tap her head and bend her knees before adding her own movement, etc.

- Throwing sounds: one person makes a sound, which a second person 'catches' by repeating it (this is best done in a group standing in a circle and enhanced if the 'thrower' and 'catcher' pretend to be throwing a ball to each other in time with the sound).

- Balloon ball: trying to keep an inflated balloon in the air by batting it upwards or between each other.

- Changing posture: every time the bell rings the participants have to change to a different posture, such as stretching, crouching, standing on one leg, looking over their shoulder, etc.

- Playing 'mindful' Jenga: try to remove a wooden brick from a tower without toppling the tower.

- Bead sorting: the therapist tips over a pot of coloured beads and the participants have to sort them into piles of different colours as quickly as possible.

- Counting backwards (if doing this exercise in a group, it can be made harder by asking people to stand in a circle making eye contact with the others as they do the exercise): the answers are chanted out loud on the beat, but each person has to start from a different number (perhaps the last three digits of their phone number). The end result is a chant where simultaneously every person says a number out loud, but it will be a different number to that of their fellow participants. This requires a great degree of mindfulness. If that's too easy you can make it counting backwards in 3s.

- Kim's game: put a display of small items on a tray – aim for about 20, and allow participants to observe it for one minute, without taking notes. Then cover the tray and ask them to write down what they remember. This can be done whether you are working one-to-one or in a group.

At the end of the participation exercise the clients are asked what they noticed – whether they were able to fully join in with the experience or whether they got distracted by the commentary of their mind.

What follows is an example of a typical client/therapist exchange after a practice.

KAREN. What did you notice during that exercise (keeping the balloon in the air)?

SEAN. I got really competitive; there was no way I was going to let it drop.

KAREN. And what happened when you had that thought?

SEAN. I was up on my toes and my heart was racing every time it went near the floor.

KAREN. So, you didn't get distracted by anything outside of the exercise.

SEAN. No, I was right in it till the end. I enjoyed it.

KAREN. What happened to those worry thoughts you had when you arrived?

SEAN. They went. But I was just distracting myself with this game. I mean, you can't do that all the time. I can't go around batting a balloon over my head all day.

KAREN. That's true. If you had spent this five-minute period worrying, what do you think the outcome would have been? Do you think you'd have solved the problem you are worrying about?

SEAN. No, my worries are not about stuff you can solve like that.

KAREN. Hmmm, this is like that chessboard question: is it black squares on a white board or white squares on a black board? Did the exercise where you batted a real balloon distract you from your thoughts, or do you think your worry thoughts often take you away from the actual experience of the moment?

SEAN. I see what you mean, but I had something to physically do in this exercise. I'm often not so bad when I keep occupied.

KAREN. Maybe you can start to notice that you are always occupied doing something, even if it is just walking, or just eating, or just sitting. You could try bringing your mind to whatever your arms and legs are doing, instead of batting that 'worry balloon' around inside your head!

SEAN.   It would help if I could. I'll have a go.

Sometimes the client cannot get themselves to do the exercise at all because of the actions of the mind. We often announce to a group that we are all going to sing for three minutes, and everyone can sing anything they want. Then as soon as this instruction is given, we say one, two, three, GO (at this point it is worth noting that very occasionally the teacher will be left singing on their own, an excellent practice opportunity for letting go of those judgements). In most cases the group will have at least one of each of the following: hearty singers, those who mumble through, those who mime and those who remain mute.

This is a fabulous opportunity for making this teaching point: "For some of you the task threw up no self-consciousness at all; for some your mind made an objection but you ignored it; for some the injunction to refrain from singing was so strong that you didn't do the task at all." It is important that the therapist is not intimidated or worried by any client not joining in the practice, and that the therapist does not take this personally or think the exercise was a failure in some way. This is exactly what we are trying to demonstrate – an opportunity to highlight to the client how much impact their mind can have on their behaviour. Just as the client avoids this experience, they will avoid others due to some action of the mind. The role of the therapist is to pick apart how that came about in this moment.

Therapists can learn a lot about themselves by doing this exercise too, and we often introduce it when we are training therapists to teach mindfulness skills. One delegate told us, "I used to get a bit frustrated with my client because there were a number of things I was sure he could do but he wouldn't even give them a try. I used to think, why doesn't he just do it? Then here today, I didn't think my singing would sound very tuneful so I just didn't sing. The strange thing was that I *wanted* to do it, but the judgement I made of myself was just so powerful." Over time we want to encourage clients and therapists to just notice the way their mind gives them instructions and to make a conscious choice to either obey them or to let them go.

Rehearsal practices

The following exercise is one of the rehearsals that we do during a session in order to encourage clients to be mindful when they get home. It works best in a group, but can just as easily be done in individual therapy with the therapist and client taking turns to speak.

THERAPIST   We are going to imagine that we are at home and we are going to make a cup of tea mindfully. This means we are going to describe all the information that we are likely to take in through our senses while we prepare the drink. I will start us off:

I am lifting the kettle off its stand and I hear a slight click as I do so. I can feel the coolness of the metal handle under my fingers and the weight of the empty kettle as I lift it. I hear my footsteps on the tiles as I walk to the tap. I flick open the lid of the kettle and it makes another click. I see the shiny silver sink and draining board. I reach in front of me, feeling the coldness and the knobbly ends of the tap, with a degree of resistance as it turns. I hear a slight high-pitched squeak and then the gushing sound of the water. I see it coming out of the tap in a swirly column of bluish grey and feel the kettle getting heavier as the water rushes inside.

> Now I am going to hand the story over to the next person, can you take up the story from being at the sink filling the kettle?

The role of the therapist as the client starts the next piece of description is to encourage the client to stay with imagining their sensations, so for example if the client says, "I get out the milk" then the therapist will prompt: "How did the bottle feel in your hand? Was there a smell as you opened the milk? Could you hear anything?" The therapist will also guide the client back to the physical sensations if they start getting caught up in judgements or thoughts.

This is one of the most popular exercises in our group, and one that seems to produce an immediate change in behaviour when clients go home and make tea after the session. Variations on the exercise can be making a bowl of cereal mindfully or brushing your teeth mindfully. Choosing something that the clients do frequently makes it more likely that they will repeat the practice.

Being open to all experiences, desirable or not

As we are encouraging clients to live their lives more mindfully it is inevitable that we will get questions about unpleasant experiences. The following story is a very gentle introduction to the concept of openness.

> I took my daughter, aged five, on the bus. She was thrilled. She loved the jostling sensation, the tickets on the floor,

the condensation on the windows, the smell of the diesel. She was fascinated by the other passengers, looking intently as each person pushed past us to get to a seat. In fact, she loved everything that I had come to hate about bus travel. What she loved, to sum it up succinctly, was the 'bus-ness' of the bus.

How sad that it should come to this. I was approaching my experience with a list of what I considered desirable and undesirable. This notion of judging the experience is not something that we are born with; children start with an interest in everything, they just seek out sensations and novelty. But as we age, we begin to become choosy, and if we are not careful, we gradually avoid a whole range of activities until only the comfortable ones are left. Our life becomes like a symphony without the low notes.

Here is another personal example that can form the basis of a discussion.

I told a friend that I would love to visit the Taj Mahal. She had been there already and told me, "You don't really want to go there – the heat, the smells, the trinket sellers pestering you to buy stuff."

But isn't that the *real* experience of going to the temple? Being there with whatever the sights, sounds and smells truly are. This is the difference between someone who has visited the real thing and someone who has only seen it, airbrushed and sanitised, in a magazine or on film.

For many of our clients the experience of their actual life is not pleasant. The things that have brought people to therapy can be painful. One of our clients was severely depressed as his wife was dying of cancer. He was admitted to hospital briefly and on discharge was referred for mindfulness sessions. He learned to notice when his mind was wandering to the future and to bring it back to this current moment, even though this was a moment of acute sadness. In doing so he was able to stay with his wife through her last days. He later recounted that some of his most tender moments with her were during that time.

The teacher of mindfulness skills needs to be confident to answer these questions: "Why would I want to be awake and alive to moments of pain and sadness? Isn't it better to mentally distance myself?"

Here are six reasons for staying with an experience, even if it is painful.

- We cannot maintain avoidance in the longer term. And when avoidance falters, as it inevitably must, we experience the impact of our pain more acutely.

- We cannot build our resilience without exposure to the situations and emotions that we dislike.

- When we fight our experience, our pain gets bigger; when we experience it, we notice it passing.

- Pain is a natural part of life, and if we try to reject it, we also miss out on meaningful activity. Our world gets smaller as we try to stay in our comfort zone.

- We cannot solve our problems if we are mentally absent.

- Pain that we willingly open ourselves to is not nearly as bad as pain we try to avoid.

We can introduce mindfulness practices in session or as homework assignments to reinforce this message. Our advice is to keep them short and simple.

- Hold out your arms in front of you (if you don't have any physical health problems that would preclude you from this practice). Notice the urge to let them drop down, but keep them straight. Instead of reacting against the discomfort, notice what it is like and see if you can stay with it longer than you would ideally like.

- Sit entirely still for five minutes. Notice any urges to move, even to swallow, and try to accept them willingly, but without acting on them straight away (it is OK to blink and to breathe!).

- Take turns saying out loud, "I am aware that when I am sad..." and add an observation.

- The next time you notice it is raining, stand for two minutes with the intention of just getting wet. Don't use an umbrella or cover your head or let your face pucker up or your shoulders rise. Just experience the feel of the rain.

- When emptying the household-waste bins, do so willingly, without trying to rush through to get it done quickly or distracting yourself with other thoughts.

In each exercise the active ingredient is willingness to accept the experience without rejecting or escaping from it. Here are some more examples to help clients understand why this is necessary.

One summer there seemed to be a particularly large number of wasps around. Whenever a window was opened to let in some fresh air in the stifling heat, within minutes a wasp would fly in. Whenever Jess and her family took a picnic to the river bank, wasps would buzz around investigating all their sugary items. Jess hated wasps and was terrified of being stung, so she spent a lot of her time ducking and shrieking and generally being pretty miserable.

Until the day she was at work and didn't notice that a wasp flew in behind her, stinging her on the shoulder. At first she was mortified, but as the pain of the sting subsided she said to herself, 'Is that it? This tiny amount of discomfort that fades in minutes? I have spent hours of my summer trying to avoid just three minutes of pain.' After that she made every effort to participate fully in the activity of the day, wasp or no wasp.

Greg was going through a court case with his previous employers. The interviews, statements and court appearances seemed to drag on forever, and when he attended court all he could think was 'I don't want to be here.' He found that his muscles were tense, and his answers were curt. He was consumed by the injustice of his position. Drawing on his mindfulness practice he decided to fully participate in the court case, despite the fact that he didn't want to be there. When he noticed himself tensing against the situation, he allowed his muscles to relax and said to himself, 'I am here, there is nowhere else for me to be right now.' Instead of having to drag his mind to the proceedings he willingly turned his attention to the person who was speaking and listened mindfully. In his own answers he gave as full and frank an account as he could. He released his attachment to things being a different way and did each task to his full capacity. He noticed that people reacted to him differently, and he felt a sense of peace with himself that he had not imagined possible in these circumstances.

The final step for clients and therapists in this journey of living more mindfully is developing the ability to discern the *richness* of our lives.

Henry was a war veteran. He was describing to his care worker some of his wartime experiences in great detail and she was engrossed in his account. He described some very traumatic experiences. As she turned to go, he thanked her for listening and told her, "Those years were the worst years of my life, and also the best. We lived with the threat of death yet I have never felt more alive. We valued everything, even the ache in our muscles felt good somehow, like we were really working at something."

Linda picked up her son from school and they walked home together. She felt his warm hand in hers, hearing his high-pitched excited voice recounting the day's activity. She felt the sun on their shoulders and noticed the smell of the still-damp poster-paint on the picture he had handed her to carry. She knew that even though tomorrow was another school day, this moment would never happen again.

Living mindfully is the recognition that what is past has gone, and what is to come may never happen. This moment is fleeting, and by being mindful we can allow ourselves to fully experience everything it has to offer.

A key skill of being fully present is noticing the little things. These exercises are popular with clients to bring home how unmindful they can be:

- Take photos of sites they are likely to have walked past around their vicinity or that of the clinic/therapy centre. Zoom in to a small detail and put these on a series of slides, or print them onto card. Ask the clients to identify where the photo was taken.

- Play the sound track to some adverts they might have seen or heard and ask them to write down the name of the product being advertised. A variation on this is to isolate the logos of popular manufacturers (cereals, shampoos, cleaning products, canned goods, cars) and ask them to name the brand.

- Put some small but familiar items into a drawstring bag and ask the clients to identify the items through touch alone.

- Get some familiar herbs or spices and cover the outside of the jar with paper so the clients cannot read or see what is in the jar. Ask them to identify the contents by the smell. Examples might be cinnamon, mint, ginger, oregano, nutmeg, vanilla pods. Teabags used to make different fruit teas can be another variation on this exercise.

There are some homework practices that can enhance the skill of living mindfully.

- Dress mindfully. As you hold each item of clothing, notice the textures and colours. Note the sensation of the clothing on your skin (some clients with sensory issues have said that they don't like the sensation of their clothing, experiencing it as scratchy or hot. But when they *willingly* turn towards those sensations, with acceptance, their relationship with the scratchiness or heat changes.)

- Walk through doors mindfully. Notice the sensation of the door handle in your hand, the weight of the door as you push or pull, notice your body going through the doorframe – at first it is in front of you, then over your head, then behind you. Notice the point at which you are dead-centre between inside and outside, or between two rooms.

- Listen mindfully. When you are with someone, put your whole attention on them and what they are saying. Don't interrupt or formulate a reply while they are speaking. Trust that when it comes to your time to talk, you will find something to say.

- Notice things growing around you. The hedges you walk past on the way to work or the shop, the weeds sprouting up through the cracks in the pavements (don't judge them for being weeds), the grass verges, the houseplants in windows that you pass.

- Be mindful of your food whether you are shopping, cooking or eating. Observe the packaging, and how it feels to the touch, notice the smell of the ingredients as you prepare your meal, notice the sensations as you eat.

- Be alert to unfinished tasks, when your mind pulls you off to something else before the job you are currently doing is complete. When you put the laundry basket down to go and check the weather for an outing tomorrow, or when you start to fill out your tax return and get distracted by some emails.

- Whether reading, watching TV or listening to music, notice when your mind has wandered, and you are no longer in contact with the text, the plot or the melody. Keep a note on your phone or on a piece of paper, of how many times this happens in a day. As you become more mindful you might notice a reduction in these unmindful moments.

Key tasks

- Orient clients to what is meant by living more mindfully.
- Give examples of being 'unmindful' in everyday life.
- Highlight to clients when their mind wanders into the past or future.
- Highlight the capacity we have to be present in our experience or to avoid it.
- Set exercises in-session and for homework to encourage mindful participation.
- Highlight how powerful the mind can be in pulling us away from fully participating.
- Orient the client to being open to the moment even if it is not pleasant.
- Set practices that encourage mindful acceptance of our current experience.

Stylistic factors

- Increase discussion of real-life scenarios and examples.
- Model being unafraid of experiences even if they are unpleasant.
- Participate fully in the exercises even if some clients don't join in.
- See non-participation of the client as an opportunity to investigate what got in the way.
- Create and collect examples, metaphors and stories that are relevant to your particular client group.

- Remember to constantly refer to how mindfulness can be used in the client's everyday life.

Bibliography

Linehan, M., 2015. *DBT Skills Training Manual*. Guilford Press.

CHAPTER 7

Acting wisely as a mindfulness skill

The concept of acting wisely and making wise decisions runs throughout mindfulness literature (Feldman and Kuyken, 2019) and practice. The mindfulness skills described in the first six chapters form the foundation for developing this skill. The first step is for clients to be aware of their thoughts, emotions, sensations and urges and to view these as passing events. This is not to say that they are unimportant, but rather that they *are* transient. By bringing them into awareness they can notice unhelpful patterns. The next stage, detailed in Chapter 6, is to be able to be fully present in the moment and participate in their actual lives. From this perspective, clients can see a range of alternatives in how to respond. They are not just reacting automatically to their experiences: they are aware of the urge to respond, and they have choices about whether or not they are making a wise decision. In helping clients to achieve this skill, clinical researchers have developed the idea of different states of mind (Linehan, 2015a, 2015b; Crane, 2017).

DOI: 10.4324/9781003386117-7

States of mind

In explaining this concept to clients, it is helpful to describe how different states of mind influence our behaviour and how we feel. In her book, Marsha Linehan (2015a) describes three states of mind: emotion mind, reason mind and wise mind. Her proposal is that emotion mind and reason mind can be helpful or unhelpful depending on the situation. Emotion mind is when emotions are driving our behaviour, whereas reason mind is the logical, rational part of ourselves. Clients can find it useful to think in terms of thoughts and behaviour coming from the heart (emotion) or coming from the head (reason). We will consider wise mind later in the chapter.

Examples of when emotion mind is effective are situations where giving an emotional response enhances the experience, such as hugging a friend who is crying or laughing aloud when watching a movie. By way of contrast, sobbing to our bank manager that we are overdrawn would probably be less useful.

Cases when reason mind is beneficial could be situations where problem solving or a 'cool head' is required, like filling out a job application or deciding on which route to take on a new journey. Alternatively, reason mind is probably not as favourable for the moment your son takes his first faltering step towards you, "Actually Johnny, strictly speaking, you're slightly behind your developmental marker for walking at this age."

The learning objective for clients is to be able to recognise which state of mind they are in and move flexibly between them. This teaching point can be tricky to convey as clients will often see one state of mind as preferable to another. The following example demonstrates this.

In discussing states of mind with her therapist, Jenny recognised that she was in emotion mind a lot of the time.

"When I'm in emotion mind I just do things without thinking. I was in the shop the other day and I felt so anxious I was sweating and thought my head would explode. I just wanted to get away so I ran out. I felt such a fool. I wish I could just be in reason mind all the time, then I wouldn't have to cope with things like that."

Jenny's therapist acknowledged that reason mind would have been valuable in that situation and took the opportunity to help Jenny weigh up the relative merits of each in different situations. Jenny was able to identify examples of when emotion mind was helpful, such as having empathy for the older people she did voluntary work with, and when it was less effective, such as being very anxious when she was taking her driving test. She also recognised that whilst reason mind was appropriate when helping her daughter with her homework it was less useful when admiring the handmade card her daughter gave her for her birthday. Through this discussion Jenny recognised that the productive thing to do in the shop was to be able to move fluidly into reason mind rather than to be permanently in a logical, rational state.

This discussion goes particularly well in a group, as clients will often differ in terms of which mind they are in most of the time. Their personal stories bring life to the discussion about when each state of mind is helpful or unhelpful.

Coach Kofi was talking to the basketball team about preparing for the game. He reminded them of the mindfulness training they had been given and the different states of mind they had talked about.

KOFI. Who finds emotion mind helpful before an important match?

ZURI. Yeh me. I get excited before a game and I feel charged, like full of energy. It helps me be quick, like super-fast.

KOFI. Anyone have a different experience?

ANIL. Yeh, sometimes I get really anxious, in case I let the team down.

KOFI. These are great examples. Emotion mind can be helpful or unhelpful. It can energise us and some anxiety is really natural. In fact, it can help us play better. The downside is sometimes our emotions can take over and get in the way of playing our best game. What about reason mind? Who finds that useful before an important match?

ANIL. I find that helpful when I'm worried. I remind myself that I have been anxious before and I have played a good game. I just need to focus on playing the game.

ZURI. Not me. If I think about it, I don't enjoy it. I play best when I just go with my instincts.

KOFI. Good job! Like I said, no right or wrong answers here. The skill is in recognising which state of mind you're in and being able to move flexibly if it's not working for you.

As mindfulness teachers our goal is to enable the client to identify each state of mind. Through discussion and feedback, they learn to recognise the cues for emotion mind and reason mind such as: the words we tend to say to ourselves; the body postures we adopt; our facial expressions and tones of voice (both internal and external). When they are able to recognise both emotion mind and reason mind, the task is to coach the client in moving flexibly between them. Often, we find that changing body posture or taking a step to one side helps to find the other perspective and answer the question, "What would the other mind say?"

Finding wise mind

Linehan (2015a) describes wise mind as taking into account both emotion mind and reason mind perspectives. It is a felt sense in that we experience it in our bodies; it *feels wise* (Gendlin, 1996). We can see why clients may have got out of the habit of trusting their instincts. Some will have a history of being abused where they were told that what they thought or felt was different to their actual experience. Alternatively, others will relate living life 'in their heads' so much of the time that they have got out of the custom of paying attention to their bodily sensations.

Sometimes clients will say they have never acted wisely in their lives and don't have faith in their ability to know what is wise. Often this lack of confidence is entirely understandable given their learning histories. In our experience, encouraging them to let go of self-critical judgements is the key. When they do this, they will usually be able to identify times when they have been wise in their actions or known what the wise thing to do was, even if they did not actually do it. Also, they can frequently identify wise advice they have given to others. It can be affirming for them to realise these are all examples of their own wise mind.

A common mistake that clients can make is deciding whether an action is wise based on the consequence. An example would be the client who is in debt and finding it hard to cover the food bills but spends £20 a week on lottery tickets. They may choose to spend less on lottery tickets so that they can buy food for the family that week. Even if the lottery numbers that they regularly choose subsequently come up, it does not make their decision to prioritise feeding the family any less wise.

If we ask a client, "Have you ever behaved in a way that you knew at the time was not wise?" they will frequently say, "Yes." This is their wise mind in action.

Steps to wise mind

Linehan (2015a) likens wise mind to a wise friend. To help clients move to this position we have identified a procedure to follow that we call 'steps to wise mind.'

- Pause.
- Ask, which mind am I in?
- Ask, what would the other mind say?
- Ask what action choices do I have?
- Ask, which of them *feel* wise?
- Be prepared to keep trying until it feels wise.
- Give it time.

We have found that clients find these 'steps to wise mind' very helpful and often like to put them on their phone or have them pop up on their computer as a prompt when they are in difficult situations.

In coaching these steps with clients, the therapist's role is to work in partnership with the client.

We have found these pointers particularly useful in coaching this skill.

- Clients will often want to rush, so helping them to slow down and reflect is important.
- In a collaborative and enquiring way notice and give feedback to the client about changes in their body posture, tone of voice and so on, to cue them into identifying which mind they are in and help them to adopt a different perspective.
- Ask the client to 'try each on for size' when they are considering their action choices, i.e., mindfully imagine they had

taken each choice, what comes up and how wise it would feel.

- Encourage them to locate where they experience the sense of being wise in their body and become familiar with that feeling.

- Encourage them to go over the steps more than once.

What follows is an example of how a staff member used 'steps to wise mind' to help her.

On her return from leave, Chloe, a fairly new therapist, found that her client (Ann) had responded very well to the locum therapist's suggestion to use mindful describing when talking to her boss about a problem. Chloe was filled with self-doubt. 'I've missed what was really needed. I'll never be a good therapist. My clients have missed out by having me as a therapist.' Chloe had been practising mindfulness and used the 'steps to wise mind' to help her think this through.

- Pause.
- *Which mind am I in?* I'm in emotion mind and it is saying, 'I'm anxious that I'm making mistakes and not doing the best for my clients. That I'll never be a good therapist no matter how hard I try.'
- *What would the other mind say?* Reason mind is saying, 'It was helpful for me to arrange for the locum to see Ann. It's useful to know that mindful describing works well for Ann as we can incorporate that into our therapy.'
- *What action choices do I have?* I could stop doing mindfulness with my clients. I could accept I'm

learning and that includes learning from others. I could do nothing and carry on telling myself off about it.

- *Which of them feels wise?* When I imagine stopping doing mindfulness with my clients or doing nothing – neither of those feels wise. When I imagine accepting learning from others it feels very different – it *feels* wise. Being concerned about doing what's best for my client shows my commitment to them. Some anxiety is natural. It is unhelpful to criticise myself for it. There will always be things I can learn from other therapists, and if I am warm towards myself and remind myself learning is a journey, I'm more able to embrace this rather than being frightened by it. It was a good call to arrange the session and I can give myself credit for this. I can keep mindful describing as a potential strategy for clients in the future and use it with Ann now.

The step of asking clients to consider their action choices and mindfully imagine what would come up with each is important, as it anchors the decision in the current context. For example, Milly is a young mum living in temporary bedsit accommodation with her baby, Topaz. She was working through 'steps to wise mind' and was at the point of discussing her action choices with her therapist, Carl.

MILLY.   It would feel wise for me to move to a house but in reality, right now, I am only being offered a flat in town or to move back in with mum.

CARL.   That's true. Why not try each choice on for size. That's where you pretend to yourself you have made the decision to move back in with your mum. What comes up?

MILLY.   I love my mum and she does help with Topaz but we argue when we spend a lot of time together, so that choice makes my stomach churn. I'm nervous it will end with me moving out again. It doesn't feel wise.

CARL.   Now pretend you have made the decision to try the flat in town, what comes up?

MILLY.   That feels so different, it *feels* wise in my gut. I can have my own space and see mum too. I can work towards a house in the future. For now, the flat *feels* like the wise choice for me and Topaz.

Another example is a client who phoned for coaching in using mindfulness skills. Lena, the client, had recently been successful in stopping drinking alcohol. She had worked hard on keeping away from situations where she encountered alcohol. She had learned and used the 'steps to wise mind' before but was struggling on this occasion. The conversation went like this:

LENA.   (Speaking really quickly.) Something dreadful happened, well something great really, but then it was awful.

ALICJA.   OK, so take a breath, slow down and describe mindfully what happened.

LENA.   I went to the social club I've been to recently and as I was leaving Ruth asked if I'd like to go for a drink with her to the new pub one evening. I really like Ruth, and I think she likes me too. I really want to say yes but I can't be around alcohol. (Talking faster.) I tried using steps to wise mind but if I say no, she'll find out all the problems I've had and then she'll hate me!

ALICJA. That's a really tricky situation and I'm pleased you called. I think steps to wise mind is a great idea. It sounds like you're caught up in emotion mind and it's hard to get out of it.

LENA. I've tried but I just keep thinking saying yes isn't a great idea but I really don't want to say no.

ALICJA. When you say "yes isn't a great idea" which mind do you think that is?

LENA. (Hesitant.) I guess it sounds like reason mind. I think it's saying being around alcohol just now could be a trigger for me drinking again.

ALICJA. I think you're right.

LENA. And emotion mind is saying "but I really don't want to say no." (Pauses.) I need a way of saying yes and not being around alcohol.

ALICJA. Hmmmm.

LENA. I guess I could suggest we go for a coffee.

ALICJA. What if she said "no," she really wants to try the new pub (troubleshooting).

LENA. Well, (thoughtful) I would be disappointed but I do know it's not the right time for me to be around alcohol at the moment and so, if that's important to her, I guess it wouldn't work out anyway.

ALICJA. Does that feel wise?

LENA. Yes, it really does.

In this example, Alicja skilfully guides Lena to recognise her reason mind and the message it is giving her. By labelling it in this way, it helps Lena to take a step back from the thoughts and emotions, recognise the truth in both sides and find her own wise solution. Alicja gets Lena to try out her decision by prompting her to consider how it would be if Ruth said no. Lena was clear about the decision she had made and that it felt wise. If the client is still unsure, suggesting they wait a while and repeat the process can be useful. If they get the same answer, it is more likely to be wise mind.

Wise mind practices

There are several practices that can be helpful in developing the skill of recognising emotion and reason mind and finding wise mind. In a group for people with learning disabilities, clients used a set of scales. They enjoyed putting weights on either the 'emotion' or 'reason' side of the scale. By standing on each side and describing what they were thinking and feeling they were able to recognise the concepts of emotion and reason mind more easily. When discussing wise mind, clients would talk about head (reason) and heart (emotion), placing weight(s) as they did so. Then they would stand in front of the scale to discuss their action choices and which feels wise, before deciding on their wise owl (wise mind) response. An important teaching point is that the scales do not need to balance, nor does there need to be an equal number of 'weights' on each side. Of course, on a few occasions this may happen, but that is not the aim. Both reason mind and emotion mind need to be considered in finding wise mind. However, some wise actions come more from emotion mind than reason mind, and vice versa.

Clients of all ages and in various settings have also found colour coding helpful when learning this mindfulness skill. Emotion mind is seen as hot and represented by the colour red. Reason mind is cool and represented by blue. Wise mind is the blend of the two and can be shown in the gradients of purple achieved by mixing blue and red. This can an engaging way of discussing the teaching point that on some occasions the wise mind blend will include more emotion mind and on others more reason mind.

Mindfulness teachers may use cards to show the colours. Sometimes they will use bottles of red and blue paint and demonstrate mixing the two colours together as shades of purple gradually appear. On other occasions it is possible for clients to have the paint themselves, describing each state of mind as they paint with red or blue and then describing wise mind as they mix the two colours together.

Keenan et al. (2023) outlined how the use of colour can make understanding abstract concepts more accessible to people who are neurodivergent. This is an important consideration and, in our experience, all clients benefit when the teaching includes different presentations and examples.

A similar practice uses coloured circles on the floor. The teacher describes a scenario that would be familiar to the clients and they stand in the 'emotion mind circle,' 'reason mind circle' or 'wise mind circle' depending on which mind they would be in. A variation of this is to ask the clients to stand in a circle and describe what kind of situation would prompt them to be in this mind state. For example, if they were stood in 'emotion mind circle' they may say, "I was sad that my cat was ill and I was worried about him" or "I was at the fair on the big dipper ride and I was so excited!"

We have seen how Marsha Linehan's concept of states of mind can be very helpful. Let us compare this with the concept of 'modes of mind' in Mindfulness-Based Cognitive Therapy (MBCT) (Crane, 2017).

Modes of mind

In MBCT different modes of mind are identified: doing mode and being mode. These do not map directly onto Linehan's states of mind but there are similarities. For instance, the aim is to develop awareness of which mode of mind we are in, and to be able to move flexibly between them. The idea is that both can be more or less helpful depending on what is happening. Awareness of the current situation opens the opportunity to think and behave differently. The idea is that in modern western cultures we spend a lot of time in doing mode and this is where problematic patterns often arise. The skill needed is to access being mode more readily and move between the two as required. Doing mode and being mode are described in more detail below.

Doing mode

Doing mode and being mode have different functions. Doing mode monitors discrepancies between how things are and how we want, or don't want, them to be (Segal et al., 2002), and it activates problem solving to reduce or maintain this discrepancy. It is goal focused, with thoughts about the event rather than directly experiencing the present. When in this mode, our attention is often on the past or future. This state of mind lacks acceptance of how things are, being mainly concerned with how to make things different.

Doing mode can be highly effective in helping us to solve problems but is less effective in helping us to experience the present as it is. If the problem we have is that we are going to see a film at the cinema but don't know when it starts or which bus is going to get us there on time, then doing mode is helpful in leading us to search the internet for the relevant websites and plan our evening. If the problem we have is that our partner of 30 years has died and we feel intense sadness and grief, then doing mode will lead us to try to reduce the discrepancy between how it is and how we want it to be. This can result in us going over and over past events, 'Why didn't I say...' or 'Why didn't I do…,' and so on. In this way we avoid experiencing our emotions, instead getting caught in a cycle of rumination on past times or feared futures. In this situation being mode is necessary to enable us to be in the experience and allow ourselves to feel the emotions that are a natural consequence of our loss.

Being mode

In this mode the attention is on experiencing the moment using all five senses: smell, touch, sight, hearing and taste. It is an important teaching point that this is not just about being in the reality of pleasant events but being present in neutral, distressing or unpleasant events too. It is about being *in* the experience of your actual life, whatever that may be. In this way being mode has a very different perspective to doing mode. Recognising our bodily sensations is an important part of this as it can provide a way to ground us in our experience and so help us to 'shift gears' into a different mode of mind. Being mode is not just experiencing our internal environment but also our external environment with information taken in through our senses (Crane, 2017).

Which mode am I in?

One way of teaching clients to recognise which mode they are in is to ask them to notice if their actions are directed towards a particular goal. Doing mode is about getting somewhere. In contrast, being mode means unhooking from the attachment to outcome. Being mode is acknowledging how things are, rather than trying to change them. It necessitates letting go of our mind's commentary on the present moment in favour of involving ourselves in the direct experience of it.

Metaphors can be really helpful in explaining the difference between doing mode and being mode. One commonly used metaphor is that of a lake. Looking from the shore we can see the water is choppy from the wind. The undulating surface is like the activity of doing mode, reflecting the constant drive to make things different that characterises this mode. In contrast, as we go below the surface to the deeper water, it becomes still and less affected by the wind. This can be seen as mirroring being mode. Both the surface and the deeper water are parts of the lake. It is not that one is good and the other bad, one right and the other wrong. Rather we are seeing the lake from different perspectives in the same way as doing mode and being mode are different perspectives on our experience.

Another metaphor that clients will often like is that of the road journey. Imagine we are driving our car, focused on our destination, our thoughts full of where we are going and how to get there. This is synonymous with doing mode. Contrast this with a trip where we are noticing the scenery when we pass, fully aware of the sights and sounds around us. This example is more akin to being mode.

In teaching these different modes of mind it is important we make it clear that the aim is to be able to intentionally switch from one to another so that we can make wise choices about how we respond to situations. Here is a personal example.

> I love watching a well-known dancing programme on TV. One evening I was sitting on the sofa at home when an advert came on giving dates for this show coming to my local theatre. Oh, be still my beating heart! I moved into doing mode. I was goal focused, my attention was on

getting in touch with my friends and organising the trip to the theatre. There was a total lack of acceptance of my current ticketless state. My focus went to the future and how much I would enjoy the show and, on occasions, to the past. Yes, you will probably have guessed that when a similar show had been on, my lack of action had led to it being sold out before I had organised my tickets. This was not going to happen on this occasion. I was determined, problem solving and action orientated.

Let's roll the clock forward to the night of the show. Imagine I am in doing mode. I arrive at the theatre scanning for discrepancies. Where are my friends? Should I have arranged to meet them here? Will we find each other in the crowds? What will we do if we miss each other when I have the tickets (no one was going to prise them from my grip until I handed them over to the attendant)? Oh, here is my group of friends, phew! Now we are at our seats and I think we will see quite well. Or would we have been better with seats in the balcony? Would my friends have preferred the view from there?

How much do we think I am enjoying the experience?

Let's imagine a different scenario. It's the evening of the show and I have found a parking space and arrived on time, thanks to doing mode. I realise that being mode will be effective in my enjoying this experience and start to focus my attention on information coming in from my senses. I notice the sense of joy as I see my friends' faces appear and the smell of perfume as we hug. I'm looking at the gold on the balcony railings glistening in the lights and the sound of the orchestra as it tunes its instruments. I'm aware of the chatter of voices and the sense of anticipation as we take our seats. I can feel the velvet on the cushion of the chair under my legs.

> Which mode do we think is more effective in this environment?
>
> But let's roll the clock back. If I had not been able to move into doing mode when the advert came on and had stayed in being mode, then I would have been acutely aware of the sadness at not having tickets and the feeling of heaviness in my heart.

So, each mode is helpful or unhelpful to us depending on the situation, and the skill we are teaching is to be able to recognise each and be able to move flexibly between them depending on what is effective in that moment.

Effectiveness

Marsha Linehan (2015a, 2015b) describes the mindfulness skill of effectiveness as focusing on what works in any given situation. She pointed out that we can get caught up in judgements about what is right or just end up 'cutting off our noses to spite our faces.' Alternatively, we can be mindful of the situation as it is, recognise the range of possibilities open to us and choose the wise response. Without this skill we can end up following well-worn patterns of thought or behaviours, which take us right back to where we don't want to be.

Another way of explaining the skill is that some events benefit if we are in doing mode and some if we are in being mode. The art is to recognise each of them. If it's effective to be in being mode, then be in being mode. If it's effective to be in doing mode, then be in doing mode. A useful question to ask is, 'When is it helpful to act (doing mode) and when is it helpful to let things be as they are (being mode)?'

In deciding whether we are taking the effective path we suggest clients ask themselves:

- Is this effective for me?
- Is this getting me closer or further away from where I want to be?

Obstacles to being effective

In teaching this skill it is helpful to highlight different types of obstacles that get in the way of our being effective. These can be:

- practical problems such as the wrong equipment to carry out a task
- intense emotions, e.g., being angry and not listening to our partner's explanation
- thoughts, e.g., 'It's impossible' or 'I may as well give up.'

In talking to his therapist about his thoughts, Tom noticed that he often had the thought 'I can't cope' when trying something new. When he had this thought he would typically give up trying and then have thoughts about being useless and a waste of space. These knocked his confidence and made it harder to try novel things. Tom had tried challenging these thoughts but could list several examples of how he hadn't coped when things were unfamiliar, such as giving up an evening course he enrolled in or going off sick within a week of starting a job. Using mindfulness, he was sometimes able to notice the thought and carry on with what he was doing but other times he found it almost impossible to continue.

In the mindfulness group Tom heard about the skill of being effective. When he noticed the thought 'I can't cope' he would ask himself whether this was making it easier for him to do the task or harder. If it was making it more difficult, then he would direct his attention to what would help in this moment. An example of this was one day when Tom was decorating his room. The paint spilled and splashed on the carpet. Immediately he had the thought 'I can't cope with this.' He had the urge to throw down his brush and give up. Being mindful he recognised that this would not be effective for him as he would then have thoughts about being a failure and useless. The effective thing to do was to clear up the paint and continue with decorating his room. He knew he would need to mindfully let go of self-critical judgements to help him keep in the moment and not in the past when the paint had spilled.

Lose awareness of the task

As a teacher of mindfulness skills, it is useful to be aware that a common obstacle to being effective is being unmindful of the task.

A junior colleague wanted to work longer hours so needed access to the building after the reception had shut. Thinking that this seemed like a reasonable request I asked the estates department to issue the necessary pass. The estates department refused. They had a quota of passes and remained adamant no more passes would be given out. I felt this was unfair and continued to argue the point. The more I pressed my view the more intransigent they became. Then I asked myself the questions:

- Is this effective for me?
- Is this getting me closer or further away from where I want to be?

I realised that I was being unmindful and had lost awareness of the task. I had made my task proving to the estates manager that they were being unfair but actually this was getting me further from my aim of obtaining a pass for my colleague. Once I recognised this I could let go of my attachment to fair/unfair and focus on what worked. I was able to be open to new solutions rather than being stuck on one path. When I did this, I was able to see that there could be other buildings and venues that my colleague could have access to after hours to work from.

A similar example can provide the opportunity for others to share times when they recognised that an attachment or judgement got in the way of being effective, or to share stories, if they have them, of when they were able to focus on what was effective in that moment.

Sometimes a client will say, "Well, leaving the party worked because then I didn't feel anxious anymore." The teacher needs to ask in a genuinely interested and curious way whether this was actually helpful for them. It may well have been, if their goal was to stay at the party and leave when they felt anxious. If their objective was to stay at the party and talk to their friends, however, then leaving the party was not useful in allowing them to do this. The skill of effectiveness would be to notice mindfully what was helping them to stay at the party even though they felt anxious.

Mindfulness practice

Here is an example of a mindfulness practice for effectiveness that we particularly like.

Each participant is given an egg and asked to balance it on its point. It is as well to note that the eggs are real and not hard boiled, so having some kitchen towel to hand is always a wise precaution. The task is to spend five minutes balancing the egg on a smooth, hard surface without breaking it or propping it up in any way. If the egg balances, the task is then to be mindful of the egg. If the egg balances and then falls, the task is then to re-balance it mindfully. If obstacles such as thoughts or emotions get in the way then just notice the obstacle and bring yourself back to the task of mindfully balancing the egg.

There will usually be an array of responses to this practice if done within a group. Some people's minds will tell them 'It is impossible' or we are 'trying to trick them,' and the message will be so strong that they may not even attempt it. Others will notice a competitive streak that makes them determined to persist and succeed. Still others will change the task to one they prefer, such as playing with the egg. This mindfulness practice can be a rich source of feedback material, helping clients to be aware of how the actions of their mind can either block or enhance effectiveness.

Key tasks

- Teach clients to recognise when they are in different modes or states of mind.

- Help clients to see when these are helpful and unhelpful.
- Teach steps to wise mind.
- Help clients to stay mindful of the task they are trying to accomplish.
- Prompt clients to be in the habit of asking themselves: is this effective in achieving my current goal?

Stylistic factors

- Encourage discussions.
- Use personal examples.
- Model acceptance of all experience, painful or not.
- Encourage and model flexibility in moving between modes or states of mind.

Bibliography

Crane, R., 2017. *Mindfulness-Based Cognitive Therapy: Distinctive Features*. Taylor & Francis. https://doi.org/10.4324/9781315627229

Feldman, C. and Kuyken, W., 2019. *Mindfulness: Ancient Wisdom Meets Modern Psychology*. Guilford Publications.

Gendlin, E.T., 1996. *Focusing-Oriented Psychotherapy*. Guilford Press.

Keenan, E.G., Gurba, A.N., Mahaffey, B., Kappenberg, C.F. and Lerner, M.D., 2023. Leveling up dialectical behavior therapy for autistic individuals with emotion dysregulation: Clinical and personal insights. *Autism in Adulthood*, pp. 1–8. https://doi.org/10.1089/aut .2022.0011

Linehan, M., 2015a. *DBT Skills Training Manual*. Guilford Press.

Linehan, M., 2015b. *DBT Skills Training Handouts and Worksheets*. Guilford Press.

Segal, Z.V., Williams, J.M.G. and Teasdale, J.D., 2002. *Mindfulness-Based Cognitive Therapy for Depression: A New Approach to Preventative Relapse*. Guilford Press.

Generalising mindfulness skills to everyday life

Case examples with detailed teaching notes

In this chapter we show how the topics discussed in this book work in action. The objective in teaching mindfulness skills, and indeed in using them ourselves, is to integrate them into our everyday lives. We have written a companion self-help guide which goes into this in detail: *Using Mindfulness Skills in Everyday Life* (Dunkley and Stanton, 2016). As teachers, our concern to accurately convey the skills can mean we forget that we also need to teach clients how to apply them in everyday situations. This point was brought home to us in a card we received from a client we had worked with. The anecdote she told makes some excellent teaching points.

DOI: 10.4324/9781003386117-8

The importance of generalising the skill

Mia learned mindfulness in our group and became very adept at using the skills in many different situations; both to be more present in her life and, when needed, to cope with challenging events. One evening she was out with her friend Ebba and Ebba's partner Liam at a local pub. As they sat down Liam described how he had had a dreadful day at work. Mia and Ebba agreed how hard that must have been and how he had done everything he could to resolve the situation. They ordered a meal and, when it came, the conversation moved on. However, Liam kept returning to what had happened at work, going over the details, becoming more upset each time he did so.

Mia did not know Liam that well, but knew that he had suffered from depression in the past and, as part of his treatment, had learned mindfulness. Very kindly she said to him, "It's really hard when something like this has happened and you are feeling so upset, my mind would keep going back over it too. I wonder if this could be a good time to use your mindfulness skills and bring your attention into having the meal right now, because going back over what happened seems to be upsetting you more and stopping you from enjoying just being at the pub with me and Ebba?"

"Oh no" replied Liam looking surprised "That's not how I do mindfulness. I go up to my room each evening for 30 minutes. Ebba knows not to disturb me, and I do my mindfulness practice and I feel a lot better."

'Well,' wrote Mia 'I'm so pleased we didn't do THAT kind of mindfulness!'

The problem here is the lack of Liam being able to generalise the skills he had learned to this new situation. Liam was clearly willing to practise, and got benefit from doing so, but when he came to a situation where noticing his thoughts as passing mental events and bringing his focus of attention into the awareness of the present conversation and meal, he was surprised at the suggestion to do so. The main teaching point is that we need to be thinking about how our clients will use this skill throughout our sessions with them. Through the examples we give, the homework practices we set, the coaching we provide, the role-plays we do and the feedback to our clients, we need to ensure they are able to know when they can utilise the skills and how to pull them out of the bag when needed. In this way our clients have choices. Once they have the skills, knowledge and ability, they can choose whether to use them or not in any given situation.

The following scenario shows how to integrate mindfulness into individual sessions with a client and help them to generalise these skills into their life. In each of the case examples presented in this chapter, the teaching points the therapist uses are in brackets, followed by a more detailed discussion of the skills used by the therapist.

Case example: Sally

It was a foggy day when Sally set off to take her son Harry to school. Suddenly Sally was aware of a flash of white to her right when a lorry pulled out of a side road and into the driver's side of her car. A passer-by pulled her son unhurt from the wreck but Sally's legs were trapped and it took hours for the fire service to cut her free. The smell of petrol stuck in her throat and made it hard to breathe, and she was terrified the car would explode.

Recovery took a long while for Sally with several operations and physiotherapy to help her walk unaided again. She would often cry with pain and frustration at how her life had changed and the fact she wasn't able to run and play football with Harry in the garden as she had before. Gradually the physical scars healed and she was able to go back to her job as a clerk in the local planning office. She worried a lot more than she had before the accident, especially about Harry. She hated it when he was away from her and was reluctant to let him go to a friend's house to play or on a trip with school.

Sally's therapist, May, suggested that learning mindfulness could help with the worry thoughts and explained that it is a way of taking control of your attention (defining mindfulness) so you can notice when your mind has gone onto worries and bring it back to what you are doing (linking to goals).

Sally was not convinced that she would be able to do this as her mind seemed to be caught in a constant stream of worries, but even a little relief sounded good and she was keen to try anything that would help. She could see her son starting to become anxious when she left him, and she did not want him to 'catch' her anxiety when he had always been such a confident little boy.

May explained that Sally would need to do mindfulness practices regularly between their sessions (importance of regular practice). She asked Sally to try to do the exercises without constantly monitoring how she was getting on (mindfulness is not meant to 'work'). Sally loved to cook and May explained that learning the skill of mindfulness was like learning to bake a cake. You need to practise and slowly it gets easier. If you are constantly opening the oven door to see if the cake is done, it will never cook properly (use of metaphor).

Sally and May started to do mindfulness practices together in the session. They began by observing a pen and using all their senses to be aware of it (mindfulness of an object). May told Sally that her mind would probably wander when she did this, and when she became aware of it, to just notice where her mind had gone and gently bring it back to the pen (normalising the actions of the mind). Sally found her mind wandering constantly and felt frustrated that she couldn't hold her attention on the pen.

"It's a numbers game," said May. "You need to be willing to bring your mind back many times and when you do this you are being mindful." Sally was relieved she was being mindful and was surprised by how much she noticed about the pen that she had never taken in before, even though she always kept it in her bag and used it several times a day. "Not only can we notice more when we are mindfully observing but we can also pay attention to what we are doing, rather than doing one thing whilst our mind is somewhere else," said May.

"Imagine you are cooking tea for Harry while he is playing at his friend's house and your mind keeps going to worries about whether he is OK, and wishing he were back. If you were cooking the tea mindfully you could notice your mind had gone to worry thoughts and gently bring it back to cooking the meal" (generalising the skill into everyday life).

Sally tried this the next time Harry was out. She paid attention to the sight, smell, sound, taste and texture of the food she was cooking and found the more she involved her different senses in what she was doing, the more she could notice worry thoughts when they came up, and bring her attention back to the meal (generalising the skill).

Sally and May began to start their sessions with a mindfulness of the breath (mindfulness of internal environment). The first time they did this Sally noticed her breathing speeded up and seemed very irregular. She could feel her heart start to race and a sense of panic begin to overtake her. As she practised more, she was able to just notice her breathing whatever it was doing (homework practice).

As Sally became more aware of her thoughts, she noticed how her mind would go down well-worn tracks, and labelling made it easier to notice and not act. May suggested she use the image of a luggage belt at the airport and notice the urge to take the baggage off, without acting on it. Just stand and watch as the bag goes past (use of metaphor).

Sally was doing the housework one day when her leg started to ache. 'If that lorry hadn't gone into me, it wouldn't be like this.'

'OK, I recognise that luggage,' thought Sally. 'Just stand and watch the bag go past.' Sally put her whole mind on the image of the bag as it went past her, watching it disappear into the distance. Then she put all her attention on the feel of the Hoover in her hand and the sound as she vacuumed the carpet and mindfully carried on with the cleaning (mindful participation). Instead of getting upset and angry as she would have done in the past, ruminating on the accident and how it had changed things, Sally felt proud of herself that she'd kept her mind on the task and finished the job (generalising the skill).

Sally noticed a positive impact at work too and was really pleased when her boss commented how she seemed so much better. By noticing when her mind wandered, she was able to bring it back and complete whatever task she was doing (generalising the skill). She felt like she was in control of her mind rather than having to follow wherever it wanted to go. She remembered May telling her that when we are being mindful, we do one thing at a time and that this is more effective than trying to do several things at once (mindfulness effectiveness skill). She found it helped to say to herself, 'In this moment I am filing' or 'In this moment I am logging the application.'

Sally noticed she felt calmer and not so jittery all the time. By observing when her thoughts were racing ahead or going into the past, she was able to bring herself into the present moment. In doing this she felt her body had come off 'red alert' and she wasn't watching for the next disaster to strike all the time.

May recorded a mindfulness body scan on Sally's phone for her to listen to. May's voice guided Sally through the different parts of her body and asked her to focus her attention on each in turn. Sally found this very hard at first. She wanted to avoid focusing on her legs because they were stiff and painful. Sally found it hard to let go of the judgements and take a kind and curious approach to the experience (non-judgemental stance). May encouraged her to treat every part of her body the same. Not to ignore or to focus on, but just to notice each part as the spotlight of her attention came to it. Sally became aware of her whole body and that there were times when the stiffness and pain varied in intensity. She stopped trying to reject noticing her legs and was able to be more accepting and kinder when experiencing them.

For Sally, part of accepting her legs as they are was noticing that sometimes she would feel sad (mindful of emotion) when the pain or stiffness stopped her from doing activities. May encouraged her to allow the sadness to come without rejecting or holding onto it. May explained, "This is the mindfulness skill of participation, i.e., being 'in' our lives even when the experience is painful or difficult because that is the reality of our life." May told her, "When we are being mindful, we allow ourselves to have the experience and also to let it go, have it and let it go."

Sally would often think of the mindfulness story that May told her: we are at the door of our house, and we welcome every visitor and let them in without judgement. "We are going to let them come and let them go. Whatever they may be: laughter, joy, sadness or pain. We treat them all the same," said May. "We are not inviting them to sit around and stay for tea, but we are just letting them in and letting them out" (metaphor/storytelling).

Skills used by the therapist

As a therapist May used a number of strategies described in this book to help Sally understand mindfulness and use it as a skill. May started by giving a simple definition of mindfulness and linking it to Sally's goal of being able to stop worrying constantly about everything. She set up realistic expectations with Sally about the importance of regular practice and told her that mindfulness is not meant to 'work.' Knowing Sally was a keen cook she chose the metaphor of baking a cake to make the teaching point that we need to unhook from outcome and be *in* the experience.

May started by introducing Sally to mindfulness of an object and chose a pen so that it would be easily accessible to Sally for frequent practice. May did the exercise with Sally and gave her feedback on her experience of it to normalise the actions of our mind. We are in it together. When Sally found her attention wandering, May pointed out that mindfulness is not about struggling with our mind; rather it is about being willing to bring it back to the focus of attention many times. May modelled a kind and curious approach to experiences without judging them as good or bad, right or wrong.

May was alert to opportunities to help Sally generalise the skill into her everyday life to help her deal more effectively with her difficulties. She used 'being mindful of an object' and the practice of noticing where your mind has gone and returning it to the task as an opportunity for Sally to try this when she was cooking tea for Harry and worrying that he was not home. May suggested labelling the thoughts and involving all Sally's senses in order to increase the impact of the current experience. This helped Sally leave the worry thoughts and return her mind to what she was doing. May set this up as an experiment to encourage Sally to be interested in, and curious about, her experiences.

As Sally became more practised in using mindfulness, May directed her to be interested in patterns of thoughts when her mind would go 'down well-worn tracks.' May encouraged Sally to use the metaphor of the luggage belt to help her not engage with the content of the thoughts and simply watch as they pass by. In this way Sally was able to learn to bring her mind back from painful memories in the past or worries about the future and engage in the experience of the moment, whether that was vacuuming at home or filing at work.

As is often the case, Sally and those around her started to notice a difference. May introduced the idea that we can be more effective by doing one thing at a time rather than trying to do many things. This can go against people's ideas about multi-tasking, so it was given as a request for Sally to notice and see what she observed.

May introduced Sally to the body scan by using a recording, as she thought Sally might benefit from being talked through the practice. She felt the recording would help Sally treat each part of her body with equanimity rather than holding on or pushing away parts of herself she didn't want (e.g., the stiffness in her legs). In doing this Sally became more accepting of her experience as it is, rather than how she judged it should be. Learning to be willing to accept her painful and uncomfortable experiences allowed Sally to be mindful of her sadness without judging it as bad, trying to avoid or hold onto it. May encouraged Sally to notice the passing of time and used a mindfulness story to help her recognise that we can be willing to have our experiences and then to let them go.

Mindfulness in a group

The case example we have just discussed looked at mindfulness incorporated into individual therapy. Teaching mindfulness skills is often done in a group setting so it is helpful to consider this as well. Groups can be useful for clients to see how they can generalise mindfulness skills. In hearing others talk about how they used mindfulness in their lives, or overcame obstacles when they tried to do so, clients will often feel encouraged to give skills a try in similar circumstances. There are a number of ways mindfulness can be included in groups, a few of which are listed below.

- Mindfulness is a core skill in Dialectical Behaviour Therapy (DBT), which includes individual and group sessions (Swales and Heard, 2016). Each eight-week skills group module starts with two sessions on the topic of mindfulness, and a mindfulness practice is held in every group.

- Mindfulness is incorporated into many fixed-term groups of around 12 sessions. These are focused on particular topics such as Cognitive Behaviour Therapy, increasing self-esteem, coping with emotions, etc. There are usually one or two sessions on mindfulness and a weekly practice.

- Mindfulness incorporated into groups specifically targeted to help with one area of difficulty, e.g., living with voices, run over 12 sessions to the protocol of Dannahy et al. (2011).

- A rolling-programme mindfulness group introducing clients to mindfulness skills over an eight-week period, which can be repeated.

The case example that follows is of a client who attended a rolling-programme mindfulness group.

Case example: Dan

As Dan walked home from the mindfulness group, he remembered how hard it had been to get to his first session. He'd become so insular since he took medical retirement from the local college that even the thought of meeting new people had made him break into a sweat. But Freddie, Dan's husband, had been keen for Dan to attend, walking with him to the first group.

Dan hadn't always been like that. As a teacher he'd been used to meeting new faces every year. He'd been happy until changes at work meant he felt overwhelmed by the expectations on him. It was as though all his knowledge and experience suddenly counted for nothing. A reorganisation deleted his role and he became very depressed. His GP referred him to the local Community Mental Health Team.

Dan couldn't remember much about the first group except that June, the group leader, had been very warm and friendly. She said it was a rolling group so people could join every week and some of the people had been there a little while. They smiled and said hello and said they'd been nervous when they started too. June explained that mindfulness is about placing you in the driver's seat, deciding where you want to put your attention (definition of mindfulness). She said our mind is like an untrained puppy running around so we do mindfulness practices to notice where it has gone and train it to come when we call (use of metaphor to aid understanding). This caught Dan's interest. His mind was always going back to what had happened at work and how unfair this was. His confidence had been knocked and he was frightened of new situations even though he longed to feel useful again (link to goals).

Dan liked the way June and other people in the group talked about using mindfulness in their own lives (self-disclosure to aid learning). It gave him ideas of how he could use it (generalisation) and made him feel like he wasn't so different from everyone else (normalising). At June's suggestion he started to talk to Freddie about mindfulness and explain what they were doing in group. They looked it up on the internet and Freddie seemed quite interested in the information. It felt good to talk to him like this (aiding generalising the skills).

Dan had been attending the group for a number of sessions and he enjoyed the rhythm of each week (structure of group sessions). They started with a mindfulness of the breath (anchoring in the present). Dan really liked this practice. It was the first one he had done and the one he used most often. When he was trying to get out and his mind was racing with worries about what he would say or what other people would think of him, he would notice his mind had gone to this and bring it back to his breath. He would observe the experience of the air entering and leaving his body and the rise and fall of his chest. He liked that he could do this wherever he was (generalising). June would often say, "sit with dignity" when they were doing the mindfulness practice to make sure she made the point that mindfulness is not about trying to relax but about noticing our experience whatever that is (distinction between mindfulness and relaxation).

After the mindfulness of the breath everyone would talk about the practice they had done during the week (generalisation). Dan had found it hard to talk at first as he worried other people would think his comments were stupid. When Dan was able to say this, he was surprised by June's response:

"That's a very mindful description. You noticed you had the thought, 'They will think my comments are stupid,' and you noticed that made it hard to speak. I wonder if you were to label it as a 'mind-reading thought' what effect that would have on how hard it is to speak?"

(Modelling interest and curiosity, mindful of thoughts and highlighting consequences.)

Dan was pleased he had been mindful. When he tried labelling the thought, he found it easier to step back from it and just speak (mindful of thoughts). He did this when he was out with Freddie and their friends and found it easier to speak then too (generalising the skill).

After discussing homework, the group would do different mindfulness practices. One week June asked if anyone could remember what judgements were. Dan felt pleased that he could tell everyone they are the good/bad, right/wrong, should/shouldn't evaluations that we make. June asked them to draw a cow mindfully and notice any judgements they were making. They laughed as they looked at the pictures at the end of the practice.

"I judged myself constantly," said Dan. "The cow was all wrong, I should be able to draw properly. Why couldn't I do it when everyone else seemed able to?"

"Do you do that in other situations?" asked June (looking for opportunities to generalise the learning from the session into everyday life).

"Yes, constantly," said Dan. "I think it got worse when I felt like whatever I did at work was never good enough. I have started judging everything I do and imagining everyone else is doing the same. I'm always telling myself it's wrong of me or I should do this or I shouldn't do that. It's so bad of me to do that all the time."

"So, you are judging your judgements," said June. "Hands up everyone who has ever done that" (normalising).

Dan was amazed to see every hand go up. "I did that too when I started to notice all the judgements I was making," said June (self-disclosure to aid learning). "We all make judgements but when we are being mindful, we just notice them and let go or restate them factually."

Lots of people in the group said they had found this hard but practice had made it easier. Dan was encouraged, especially when Terry told the group he had recognised he often judged himself and others. When he noticed this and began to drop the judgements, he was less irritable, which meant he got on better with people, including his husband (highlighting consequences of non-judgemental stance).

The last practice in the group each week was a mindful participation. The first time they had done this Dan realised he hardly ever lost himself in an experience. He was constantly evaluating how he was doing, guessing what others were thinking of him, listening to the running commentary of his mind (bringing into awareness). Gradually he had started to be able to practise making a cup of tea mindfully, eating mindfully, walking mindfully, brushing his teeth mindfully (mindful participation and generalising). As he got more practised he realised how much of his life he had been missing by living with memories and regrets from the past, predicting what would happen in the future or paying attention to his mind's constant chatter rather than being in the present experience. He noticed that one of the times when it was easy to lose himself in what he was doing (mindful participation) was when he was teaching and he started to volunteer at a group for helping adult learners to read (generalising the skill in everyday life).

Being in the present wasn't always pleasant, like when he and Freddie sat and cried at the impact his difficulties had had on their relationship (mindful of emotion).

In using mindfulness Dan was able to have the experience and let it go without it becoming overwhelming (generalising). He and Freddie were building their relationship again and he felt he knew himself better for all he had been through.

In the last group Dan thanked everyone for all he had learned from them. Some group members agreed to meet for a mindful walk in a few weeks' time (generalising). Dan volunteered to lead a practice and did a mindfulness of pebbles that he had collected on the beach with Freddie. He noticed the association when his mind went to the walk they had been on and gently brought it back to the pebble. As they left the room he turned to Tom, a nervous looking teenager who had started that week, and said, "I found it hard at first but do keep coming. It's made a big difference to me."

Skills used by the therapist

In this case example June used strategies described in previous chapters to help clients learn mindfulness skills in a group setting. The group was run as a rolling programme so members could join each week. Clients were asked to stay for eight weekly, one-hour sessions and could repeat this if they were finding them helpful. In total, clients could attend for eight or 16 sessions.

With clients potentially changing quite frequently the presence of June each session provided continuity. The advantage of having a rolling programme is that there was no wait to join and clients who were new to mindfulness could mix with those who were more experienced. Established participants can be very helpful in encouraging new members or those struggling to grasp a particular aspect. It can be far more powerful for another client to say they have found a strategy helpful or describe how they used mindfulness, rather than the therapist doing this.

June involved clients in running the groups by encouraging experienced members to lead a mindfulness practice. June would ask them to think about the practice beforehand and talk through it with her so she could help them plan, for example to ensure that they were only asking people to do one thing at a time. June would then take feedback from the group as described in Chapter 4, so that she could highlight teaching points.

Clients were assessed for therapy (including risk of harm to self or others) and offered a place in the group if it was seen as appropriate to the formulation and treatment plan for that individual. The therapist doing the assessment would describe the group and why it could be useful to the client. Thus, in the first session of attendance June was able to keep her orientation to a minimum. Nevertheless, she always provided a brief definition of mindfulness using a metaphor to demonstrate the point and included a statement of how mindfulness might link to goals. The repetition when new people joined encouraged more established members to keep their goals in mind and think about how mindfulness could be helpful to them.

June used appropriate self-disclosure in the group to normalise the actions of the mind and to show how she generalised mindfulness into her everyday life. She also encouraged clients to participate through feedback of their practice during the week and group discussion. In this way clients learned, from hearing the experience of others, how they could generalise the skills to situations outside of group. June also encouraged generalisation by suggesting group members look at information about mindfulness on the internet, TV and books such as the self-help guide *Using Mindfulness Skills in Everyday Life* (Dunkley and Stanton, 2016). June took advantage of mindfulness currently being a hot topic in the media to stimulate interest and share information about resources, such as a phone application of a mindfulness bell that could be set to ring occasionally and prompt a few mindful moments.

Each week June followed the same structure in group:

- mindfulness of the breath
- homework feedback
- mindfulness practice, e.g., of a: leaf, picture, spaghetti, flower, bubbles, thoughts, etc.
- mindful participation, e.g., mindful: jenga, singing, mirroring, noticing the colour blue, copying a clapping pattern, dancing etc.
- agree practice for the coming week.

June started the group sessions with a mindfulness of the breath as this is a ubiquitous mindfulness exercise which can be extremely useful in a variety of situations. By paying attention to body posture June used the opportunity to remind group members that mindfulness is not relaxation. She emphasised the distinction, so that clients would not see the aim of mindfulness as being to calm or relax them but rather to bring their experiences into awareness without judgement.

The group would feedback on their practice over the last week. In doing this June looked for opportunities:

- to point out when they had been mindful
- to help them problem solve any obstacles that got in the way of doing the practice
- to encourage all feedback, modelling an interested and enquiring stance
- to generalise learning to everyday life.

When Dan told June about the 'others will think I'm stupid' thought, she used the opportunity to point out he was being mindful in bringing this into awareness and encouraged him to notice the consequence on his desire to speak. She then took the learning a step further by suggesting he could try labelling the thought and set up an experiment for him to notice if there was any difference. When Dan fed back that he had practised with friends, it not only gave Dan the opportunity to celebrate his success but also enabled others in the group to learn from his experience.

When June introduced the topic of judgements, she asked if any group member could describe what judgements are. This served the function of checking out what group members' understanding was so she could assess whether they were developing accurate knowledge. June chose drawing a cow for the practice, as she knew people often make judgements about their drawing ability and also the drawings can be amusing. She used humour to create a learning environment for discussing judgements, which are an aspect clients often struggle with.

June made the following teaching points.

- We all make judgements, and the idea is not to judge ourselves for doing this.

- When we are being mindful, we notice when we make judgements and let them go or factually restate them.

- There is a link between judgements and emotion, e.g., Terry said he noticed his irritation went down when he became aware of his judgements and was able to drop them.

- Being less irritable had a positive impact on Terry's relationships.

June made the last practice in each session mindful participation. Sometimes this was set for homework to enable people to build the skill of being present in the current moment, whether that is being mindful of emotion and sharing sadness with their partner or recognising when they find it easy to be present in the moment. In taking feedback, June was able to encourage Dan to look for opportunities to take this learning into his everyday life. As a result, Dan recognised he found it easy to be fully present when teaching and started voluntary work helping adults to read.

When finishing the group, June encouraged clients to think about how they would continue to use the skills they had learned. In this discussion, Dan and some other group members decided to meet on a self-help basis and go walking mindfully. June told members who were leaving that they could lead a mindfulness practice if they wanted to. This was an opportunity for June to talk through the aims of a practice and help them think about continuing this when they no longer had the prompt of the group. Often clients chose to share their experience of doing mindfulness to benefit new members and as a way of saying goodbye to the group.

Mindfulness in an individual therapy session

This vignette gives a snapshot of an individual therapy session where a client has learned mindfulness and is applying this to a specific situation. The example describes in detail how teaching and practice *in* the session can explicitly show the client how to use the skills *out* of the session. In addition, it gives the client the opportunity to practise what to do when judgements get in the way of skilful behaviour. Sophie lives in a hostel but is moving out into her own flat. She has had problems with drinking in the past but her goal is to refrain from drinking. We join the therapy session at the point at which Stan, the therapist, and Sophie, the client, are exploring an episode during the week when Sophie had been drinking.

Case example: Sophie

STAN. So, let's recap: you got back to the hostel after going with your care coordinator to view the new flat you've been offered. You were watering your plants and thinking how they would look when you plant them out in your own garden, and you felt happy. Then you noticed some other thoughts? (Prompting bringing thoughts into awareness.)

SOPHIE. Yes, I was thinking that I don't even know why I'm letting myself get excited; I will only fall out with the neighbours. I'll just mess it up; I always do. It will all go wrong. (Mindful description of thoughts.)

STAN. OK, and then your emotion changed to sadness, and that's when you had the first drink? (Highlighting the consequence of the thoughts.)

SOPHIE. And I feel really disappointed by that as I haven't been drinking at all lately. (Linking with goals.)

STAN. Yes, you have done well, so I can understand your disappointment. Let's see if we can work out how we might have done this differently. Did you think of anything that might help?

SOPHIE. Well, I thought of those mindfulness skills we've been learning. I thought I could have watered my plants mindfully but I only thought of it afterwards. (Identifying potential to use mindfulness skills.)

STAN. I think you're right; they might have helped here. Why don't we practise now? Imagine yourself back watering your plants – you're going to have to talk me through what you notice as you pay attention to those plants. We've done this type of 'imagination' rehearsal before, so you know how to think yourself back to that moment in time. As you talk me through your actions, I'm going to say aloud those thoughts that were bothering you, and you are going to just notice them and gently bring your mind back to the plants. Remember to describe what you can see, or hear, or smell, or feel. (Therapist instructs client in how to notice where her mind has gone and to bring it back to the focus of attention.)

SOPHIE.   Er... OK... this is going to be hard, but I'll give it a go. *Client pretends to be watering some plants.* OK, I'm paying attention to the stream of water coming out of the spout and hitting the leaves. I can feel the watering can handle, and it's cold.

STAN.   I'll just mess it up. (Therapist interrupts, speaking out loud one of the problematic thoughts that the client had identified.)

SOPHIE.   I really will, that's what always happens.

STAN.   OK, did you notice that you just got right back into that thought? Remember that we are going to use mindfulness instead, so the idea is to just notice the thought, then quickly turn your mind back to the plants. Would it help to say, "that's a thought?" (Highlighting getting caught up in the content of the thought and suggesting labelling, modelling a light and easy tone.)

SOPHIE.   Yes, that might help, but it's still going to be hard.

STAN.   You're right, these are really sticky thoughts. (Use of metaphor.) It can help to use a light tone of voice. Mindfulness is friendly and curious, not telling yourself off.

SOPHIE. OK, I can see the water trickling down the leaves and smell the soil as it gets damp.

STAN. It will all go wrong. (Therapist plays the part of the thought.)

SOPHIE. Er... that's just a thought... I can see the pink petals of the flower moving as I pour water around the base.

STAN. Well done, you didn't get caught up in it that time.

SOPHIE. It helped to say, "that's a thought" and to make my voice a bit friendlier.

STAN. One more try?

SOPHIE. OK, it's getting easier... I can hear the trickle of water going into the pot.

STAN. I'll mess it up.

SOPHIE, *more confidently and kindly*. That's a thought... I can feel the watering can getting lighter as I pour. (Practising labelling the thought and bringing her attention back to watering the plant.)

STAN. Great, you did really well. Do you think if you had used mindfulness that evening it might have helped you at all?

SOPHIE. Yes, definitely. I'm just going to have to remember to do it.

STAN. It's like a mental muscle. (Use of metaphor.) The more you practise being mindful in your everyday life, the more you are likely to do it when you really need to. (Highlighting the importance of practice to generalise the skill.)

In this instance Stan chose to coach mindfulness skills rather than go down the route of helping Sophie to challenge her thought. This is because Sophie might well have been able to give plenty of evidence of having fallen out with her neighbours in the past. In fact, recalling her past failures may have triggered further ruminations about them. By using mindfulness Sophie did not have to engage with the content of the thought at all. In employing a role play, Stan was able to directly engage Sophie in generalising the use of the skill to her home environment. By coaching Sophie in labelling the thought and softening her tone of voice, he helped her to increase her effectiveness in using the skill.

Coaching mindfulness on the phone

Just as the pandemic promoted the use of online sessions described in Chapter 9, so it also encouraged the use of the telephone. Phone coaching has always been part of DBT, with Marsha Linehan (1993) describing how important it is to provide telephone contact with clients to coach skills, including mindfulness. Whether the phone session is planned or available ad hoc, we have found that it can really help clients to implement mindfulness in situ. The phone session may be by text or by talking on the phone. A combination of both often works well.

Chike had been learning mindfulness skills and his teacher (Akpan) offered brief phone contact to coach skills between sessions. The contact could be to let Akpan know Chike had used a skill and it had gone well, or to get help in which skill to use or how to use it. Chike had a homework assignment for school and it was due in the next day. He had put off the assignment several times, now the deadline was approaching. Every time Chike sat down to type, he'd think: 'Why didn't I do this before? It's so stupid of me to leave it so late. I'll never be able to finish it now. It will be rubbish, so why even bother?' He felt really angry with himself. His hands balled into fists and he had the urge to slam the laptop shut and walk away. He tried to mindfully take deep breaths and focus on typing the words but the same thing kept happening. After a while he texted Akpan to explain how he was struggling and Akpan phoned him back.

AKPAN.   Sounds like you're having a tough time. I'm not going to pretend it's ideal leaving an assignment to the last minute, but you know Chike, you're not the first person to do it and I'm guessing you won't be the last either. It's great you are trying to do it now, but it sounds like lots of judgements and feeling angry with yourself is getting in the way. (Summarises and models a kind acceptance to the experience.)

CHIKE.   I've tried the cloud thing and the stream (use of metaphor). It works for a while but then I get a thunder storm or a tsunami and the thoughts just keep rushing back. It makes me so angry. I'm so stupid, why didn't I do this assignment before?

AKPAN.   It's natural for emotions to run high when you have a deadline tomorrow but what happens when you judge yourself like that? (Labelling judgements and the consequences of judging.)

CHIKE.   I get more angry (mindful of emotions), and then I just want to give up (noticing urge).

AKPAN.   That makes sense, the judgements lead to feeling angrier with yourself and then you have the urge to quit. It's great you tried the metaphors and that they helped for a short while. How about you try mindfully describing without the judgements and see what happens. (Summarises and suggests mindful describing as a potential skill.)

CHIKE. Hmm, I'm angry with myself because I left my assignment until tonight (describes mindfully).

AKPAN. Anything else?

CHIKE. I'm anxious it won't be very good and I'll get a low mark.

AKPAN. Can we be a bit more specific about 'very good'? (Noticing the judgement and coaching a more mindful description by stating the judgmental thought more factually.)

CHIKE. I'm anxious it won't be very detailed because I don't have much time and I'll get a low mark.

AKPAN. That's a very mindful description, how does that feel? (Directing attention to the consequences of taking a non-judgemental stance.)

CHIKE. A bit calmer. Yeh, I don't feel so angry with myself or anxious about my work when I stop judging.

AKPAN. OK, so have you thought of anything else that could help?

CHIKE. I did wonder if I should ask for an extension. You know, that wise thing. What choices do I have?

AKPAN. I agree. I think that could help. Do you remember the steps to wise mind?

CHIKE. I think so. Emotion mind is panicking the assignment won't be very good and angry with myself for leaving it. (Takes a deep breath) And reason mind is saying at least I'll have something to hand in. Or I could show my teacher what I've done and ask for an extension to the end of the week.

AKPAN. Great. Have you tried out each choice to see what *feels* wise? (Prompting 'steps to wise mind.' See Chapter 7.)

CHIKE. I think if I do the assignment tonight, I will need to notice the judgements and say what I mean to myself, without judging. That will be hard. Heh Akpan, do you remember that balancing the egg mindfulness? I got really angry when my egg didn't balance. I just wanted to smash it, so I stopped trying. I think this is the same – getting angry is stopping me from doing the assignment.

AKPAN. Oh yes. That's a good shout. Do you think reminding yourself 'the assignment is like the egg' would help? (Use of metaphor.)

CHIKE. (Laughs) Yes!

AKPAN. How does that choice feel?

CHIKE. Pretty wise.

AKPAN. What about asking for an extension?

CHIKE. I can imagine my teacher may say no. I've been late with work before and he said next time that happened he'd give me no marks. He's pretty straight, so I think he meant it. If I showed him what I'd done so far, I think he might say I could have to the end of the week. I think seeing I'd done some would help. That feels kind of wise too.

AKPAN. Which felt most wise in your body? (Helping client to identify the wise mind decision.)

CHIKE. (Pauses) I think I could do both. Get what I can done on the assignment today (smiling) – it's only an egg – and then take it in tomorrow and, if I've not finished, show him what I've done and ask for an extension. That feels most wise.

AKPAN. Sounds like a plan. Well done. Text me to let me know how you're getting on and next session we can have a look at why assignments keep getting left so they are late or there is a rush at the end.

CHIKE. That would be cool. I'll text you.

Skills used by the therapist

Akpan kept the phone contact brief and focused on coaching the skills needed. He started by summarising the problem to check his understanding and to model a mindful, accepting approach. He normalised the experience and helped Chike to notice judgements and the consequences of judging himself in this way. Akpan highlighted the increase in emotion leading to the urge to quit as he knew recognising this link is important for many clients, including Chike. Chike had already tried noticing the thoughts and letting them go (using the metaphors of leaves floating on a stream and clouds drifting across the sky) so Akpan suggested mindfully describing without judgement and helped Chike to restate the judgemental thoughts more factually. When Chike did this, Akpan drew his attention to the consequence of a non-judgemental stance. In this way, Chike could see how the judgements impacted on his emotions and urges to act.

Rather than making suggestions, Akpan checked if Chike had any ideas himself. This helps with generalisation, as Akpan will not always be there to suggest mindfulness skills. Similarly, Akpan encouraged Chike to go through the steps to wise mind, only prompting when necessary.

Given that Chike remembered the egg metaphor himself, and the use of metaphor had helped somewhat before, Akpan suggested using the metaphor of the assignment being like an egg to help in completing Chike's work. From experience, Akpan knows that a slightly humorous image can help to lighten the tone and loosen the attachment to the content of the thoughts, making it easier to let the judgements go. (Balancing an egg mindfulness practice, described in Chapter 7.)

Akpan asked Chike to let him know how he got on, leaving the door open if Chike needed more help, whilst showing genuine interest and curiosity in the outcome of Chike using the mindfulness skills. Akpan also picked up on the need, in a future session, to see what was getting in the way of Chike completing assignments on time.

In a short phone contact, Akpan helped Chike to see what skills he could use in this situation and how he might implement them. By Akpan following up with him at the next session they were able to evaluate whether the skills had been effective (they had!) and how Chike could prompt himself to use them in future. Chike put a small wooden owl on his windowsill to remind him of wise mind. Akpan knew Chike enjoyed art so he encouraged him to find an image that would prompt using mindfulness skills. Chike made a picture of two eggs in his notebook. One was smashed and had 'given up' under it. The other was whole and had 'keep going' above it. He kept the notebook in his school bag.

Conclusion

These case studies have shown how the topics in this book come together to enable people to learn mindfulness skills and use them in their everyday lives. Whether this is done in an individual, group or telephone setting, our experience is that using these skills has often had a profound impact on people, enhancing their ability to deal more effectively with the problems they encounter.

Key tasks

- Provide a description of mindfulness.
- Use metaphors.
- Link to goals.

- Vary practices.
- Highlight new learning.
- Look for opportunities to generalise this into everyday life.

Stylistic factors

- Encourage exploration of mindfulness, for example in media and books.
- Foster sharing, e.g., of information about resources and experiences of using mindfulness.
- Welcome all feedback, using it as an opportunity to shape mindfulness.
- Model a kind, curious and accepting attitude towards all experiences.

Bibliography

Dannahy, L., Hayward, M., Strauss, C., Turton, W., Harding, E. and Chadwick, P., 2011. Group person-based cognitive therapy for distressing voices: Pilot data from nine groups. *Journal of Behavior Therapy and Experimental Psychiatry*, *42*(1), pp. 111–116. https://doi.org/10.1016/j.jbtep. 2010.07.00

Dunkley, C. and Stanton, M., 2016. *Using Mindfulness Skills in Everyday Life: A Practical Guide*. Routledge. https://doi.org/10.4324/9781315676326

Linehan, M., 1993. *Cognitive-Behavioral Treatment of Borderline Personality Disorder*. Guilford Press.

Swales, M.A. and Heard, H.L., 2016. *Dialectical Behaviour Therapy: Distinctive Features*. Taylor & Francis. https://doi.org/10.4324/9781315544540

CHAPTER 9

Adapting mindfulness skills for different settings and client populations

Since the first edition of this book came out the world has undeniably changed. Not least due to a worldwide pandemic. For a time, everybody had to be acutely mindful – where we were standing, what we were touching, where we were going, and with whom.

A side effect of the pandemic was the rocket-boost this gave to the technology that underpins online teaching. Schools, universities, evening classes, church services, keep-fit classes and therapy groups all began offering an online version, and many of them have not returned completely to face-to-face work. Online working has brought new opportunities to many, removing the stress of the daily commute, opening more jobs to people with disabilities or home responsibilities. At the same time, it has challenged mindfulness teachers to think about how we adapt our very physical practices to the online community. In this chapter, we will share some of our learning from that journey.

DOI: 10.4324/9781003386117-9

Also, in this chapter we are going to answer some of the many queries that have been posed to us by correspondents who have read the original book. They have mostly been about how mental health professionals can adapt to their specific clinical population or setting, whether that be a prison or mother and baby unit, a school, or an eating disorder clinic. We will not be summarising ten years of developments for each topic, as there have been huge amounts of work done by our colleagues in those areas. Instead, we will focus on how you can take what is already in this book, and translate it to the new setting as easily as possible. We will focus on what the obstacles could be and how to overcome them, or some additional factors you may need to consider to increase the likelihood the teaching points are well-received.

Adapting to an online delivery

During the pandemic we started with rudimentary online tools, whilst the expansion of platforms like Zoom and Microsoft Teams began improving our ability to engage with clients in cyberspace. Those who need mindfulness skills are often beset by free-floating anxiety – making driving, parking or taking public transport to get to class an additional burden. These clients were glad of the online provision, and we have seen some groups get better attendance as a result.

However, there are also those clients who hate the exposure of being on camera. For those, some platforms have an option to *hide self-view*. This means that the teacher, or other participants, can see them but they cannot see their own image on screen. For some it takes away the distraction of scrutinising their face while trying to practise the exercises. They can also blur their background if they are worried about showing their personal surroundings.

If clients have a problem being on screen the answer is not to turn their camera off. This makes it hard to see if someone leaves the room, especially if there are safety concerns. One option is to have the camera pointed at the client's profile rather than full-face. A side view makes it less intrusive for them, but still gives the therapist more idea of how they are doing. Another idea is to have the light behind the client so their face is not so brightly lit.

Online groups can still feel impersonal. At least one home visit can really help foster a better connection if this is geographically feasible.

Dana suffered from anxiety and was referred to an online mindfulness class run by her local mental health team. The clients were told that at some stage during the first term they would receive a home visit by one of the two teachers. When the instructor Harpreet called round, it was quite strange, as Dana was not used to seeing her in person.

Although group was not in progress during the visit, they sat together in front of the computer and Dana explained how she would prepare for the meeting by gathering any materials needed, having a notebook and pen, and a cup of tea.

Harpreet got a really good sense of Dana's physical environment and had little glimpses into her preferences. Dana reflected that having Harpreet physically in her home, even though it was only once, made it feel much more personal when she attended subsequent online classes. She could almost feel Harpreet in the room beside her during the session.

Be aware that socially there are fewer opportunities to get to know people online. In a physical group people chit-chat as they arrive. They might also convene in the break or walk to the car park or bus together afterwards. Online participants have complained that sessions end so abruptly. One minute the group is in full flow, and the next they are thrown back to being alone, which can be a harsh contrast. To compensate, online hosts can keep some chat time at various points during the session, and ask people to drink their teas and coffees together instead of wandering off. The link can also be held open a little before and after the session, to encourage interaction as people arrive and leave gradually, as would happen in a face-to-face environment.

A number of exercises can transfer easily online, for example mindfulness of the breath, or a body scan. Some need more setting up. To do the observation of a leaf or a pine cone, the therapist needs to instruct the client ahead of the session to have the item(s) ready. Leaves are still a favourite, and they can be found in the garden, in pot plants, in the vegetable rack or in the fridge.

Here are some more exercises that lend themselves well to online groups. They invite people to be more mindful of their environment. This is a great advantage of online working, there is no difficulty transferring the skill from the therapy room to home or work – they are already there.

1. Find the oldest object they can show on screen (pets and people not allowed!). Remember that dates can be found in books and on coins. Some people have produced jars of spices from their kitchen cupboards that are way past their sell-by date.
2. Wander round the home and look for things that have wheels (when taking feedback if people say there wasn't anything remember kitchen drawers, the dishwasher, the vacuum cleaner, kids' toys, casters on furniture, luggage).

3. Asking people to fill a glass or cup with as many green items as they can.
4. Observing practices of common items at home, a tube of toothpaste, a teaspoon, a vegetable or fruit.

Describe practices can go well, as either clients can describe things off camera that the listener has to guess or, for example, hold something with an odour (candle, lemon, perfume, soap, shampoo, disinfectant) and describe it to the others.

Some teachers have felt challenged when putting game-type participation practice into an online group. These can still be done in breakout rooms. The practice of having names shown under the thumbnail is beneficial, as it helps those who struggle to remember names. Games that require turn-taking – such as telling a story one word at a time, or memory games like 'I went to market' where shopping items are added by each participant – need a little more planning online, because the order that people appear on screen is not the same for everyone. This can be overcome by asking clients to take turns alphabetically by first name.

If the mindfulness teacher decides to 'pop in' to breakout rooms to see how participants are getting on, they should be aware of the 'shock' effect of a new face appearing suddenly, looming on screen. In our experience everything stops at that point, so do warn people before the exercise starts.

Since discovering the accessibility of online therapy there has been a demand for the best-of-both-worlds option, where a teacher can be in the room with some people and have others join online. On the whole we have yet to discover a hybrid model that does not disadvantage the online participants, whereas wholly online or wholly in person groups do well. If you are using a hybrid model it is worthwhile having a colleague monitor the online 'chat' so they can bring questions, points and discussions to the attention of the teacher. It is also worth remembering that going from an online group to meeting in person, people can come across quite differently. If you are planning that move, allow extra socialisation time to cover the transition.

Adapting mindfulness for adolescents

We have heard therapists say, "Adolescents aren't interested in mindfulness." In fact, adolescents have as much need of this skill as anyone else. Their hormones can make it very hard to move their attention away from emotionally evocative stimuli, for example ruminating about a friendship breakdown during their history lesson.

If the word mindfulness has been given a bad reputation, you can call it attentional control, or Minding your Mind. As with all clients, showing how mindfulness can be of benefit is key. Our top tip is to choose relevant examples and accept what you can get. If a young person is willing to give the therapist any air-time at all, it's a win.

> HOSE.   How did you get on with that practice of observ-
> ing the leaf?
> FREYA.   I hate leaves. They get bugs on. Can I go now?
> HOSE.   When we're done, sure you can. But before you
> do, can you tell me, does it ever happen that you start
> thinking of things your friends have said or done that's
> REALLY annoying and you can't get it out of your head?
> FREYA.   (Rolls her eyes.) If someone annoys me, I move
> on.
> HOSE.   And is it easy to forget about it? Or does it come
> back in your mind?

FREYA.   (Shrugs. Slouches back in the chair.)
HOSE.   Just if remembering it is annoying you, and you
    want to move your attention away, mindfulness gives
    you a bit more power. It's the skill of moving your mind.
    (Shrugs) You might not be interested, though… I'm not
    here to make your life worse.
FREYA.   (Sighs. Pouts, folds her arms.) Go on then.

Young people may not like to be caught in an eye-lock, so it
is better to sit side by side or if facing them, look away more.
They can dislike pressure, so avoid being intense about anything.
A take-it-or-leave-it attitude can make it more likely they will
engage than a hard sell.

If you are working in person, getting out of the therapy room
into the outdoors is really beneficial, as has been exploited by
Forest Schools. One group of Eco Sensory therapists we know
get clients to lie on their front on the grass, then dig a little hole
for their nose, and mindfully smell the earth. They also ask clients to create pictures outside from natural objects like leaves,
twigs, petals and stones. This kind of activity can appeal to adolescents who might need something out of the ordinary to keep
their attention.

Giving young people ownership of a mindfulness class can
work wonders. Ask them to look up exercises for the group on
the internet, or plan them in pairs. They can lead practices,
with preparatory guidance, while the feedback is done by the
therapist for shaping purposes. Tech-savvy young people can be
amazing at sourcing memes and animations on the internet to
support learning.

A very popular practice for adolescents has been mindful
colouring. On the one hand, anything that improves the ability
of young people to focus their attention is helpful, on the other

hand there is a danger that this is used at times of stress as a form of avoidance.

> For example: Evie got home from school and found her mind returning to a mistake she made in maths in front of the class, which was embarrassing. She decided to do some mindful colouring. This was a good use of mindfulness, helping pull her attention away from something that served no useful purpose, onto the artwork she was creating.
>
> In contrast, when Tad came in from school his mum told him he needed to call his dad, but he didn't want to as he knew his dad had found out he was using cannabis. He didn't want to tell his mum. So, he did some mindful colouring. In this case he was using colouring to distract from something he needed to address.

A classroom format can be off-putting for young people. A mindfulness class can make subtle differences from school, such as sitting on the floor and/or having snacks for the breaks. Peer pressure is often a motivator for young people, so if you are struggling to teach a client one-on-one, consider a group. The more people, the more engagement you are likely to get, and the less attention goes on the clients who don't join in. Take non-participation in your stride.

> After a game of mindful Jenga, Wade took some feedback from the class of teens.
>
> WADE. (Smiling) Oli, I notice you stopped playing the game?
> OLI. I didn't like it.

WADE. (Does not change his expression.) OK, and how did not liking it show up, was it like a feeling in your body or a thought?

OLI. A feeling, I just wanted to sit down.

WADE. You noticed an urge? And did you act on that straight away?

OLI. Not straight away, no. I kept going a bit, then I thought 'it's rubbish.'

WADE. So, until you had the thought, 'It's rubbish,' you kept going?

OLI. Just a bit longer.

WADE. Well done, it's actually quite hard to keep going if you have thoughts like, 'it's rubbish.' No wonder you had the urge to sit. Does anyone else have that thought sometimes? That they don't want to do something because of the thought 'it's rubbish?'

In the snippet above Wade keeps his tone light and gets in two learning points – firstly that Oli did not have to act on the urge immediately, and secondly that 'It's rubbish' is a thought, but one that is hard to resist. He then takes the heat off Oli by asking the others a question. Despite not participating for long, Oli has still had a learning opportunity and does not feel excluded from the group.

You might remember yourself playing 'Buzz,' a game where each young person says the next number in sequence but substitutes the word Buzz for any number that contains 7 or is a multiple of 7. If they make a mistake they drop out. This and any other 'drop-out' game can add extra value to participation exercises. Any young person who drops out is instructed to *distract* the others by waving or saying the wrong number to them (but not touching them). This is a metaphor for having to remain mindful even in the presence of problematic distractions. We would recommend you get hold of a book of drinking games, as they revolve around trying to be mindful during increasing intoxication, and translate really well into participation practices, without the alcohol, obviously!

A meta-analysis of mindfulness-based programmes for young people (Dunning et al., 2022) has shown that they increase mindfulness skills and cognitive functioning whilst reducing anxiety. The authors note that younger children may only be able to manage concrete behaviours (e.g., mindful walking) where older children can cope with more complex tasks like observing their thoughts. The meta-analysis showed that benefits did not seem to be sustained at the follow-up stage. This could be due to a lack of prolonged practice when the programme is over, as young people coming out of regular treatments have other things that take up their time, or that they drop the practice when they no longer feel they need it.

Adapting mindfulness for forensic or secure settings

As mindfulness is an acceptance strategy there is no setting more worthy of its benefits than a prison. The clients have to accept multiple losses and a myriad of restrictions over which they have little control.

Most of the suggestions we make in this book work as well in in-patient environments as they do in the community. However, in prisons and some secure hospitals, there are restrictions on what can be brought into the environment for practical practices. For example, in some settings clients might not be allowed a pen as it could be used as a potential weapon, or natural objects that could be swallowed or thrown. Some practitioners have felt uncomfortable doing body scans with sex offenders, which is a consideration. For these reasons, the most researched mindfulness practices have tended to be observing the breath or versions of yoga. A systematic review has shown that these are beneficial to well-being, with programmes running over a longer period with less intensity being more helpful than short-term interventions (Auty et al., 2017).

Teaching on the hoof, or looking for ways to incorporate mindfulness into the usual routine, can be an easier path for teachers than a formal group. A short practice of observing the breath can be added to the end of the community meeting; the end is preferable as people can leave if they do not want to participate. The option to *not do it* is important for detained patients, as they have enough mandated activity.

The first 24 hours of incarceration can be a great place to begin, as this is a risky time for suicides, especially if this is a first imprisonment. We have taught groups of prison officers in the highest secure prisons in the UK and they tell us this is often a time when the new prisoner is open to suggestion.

PRISON OFFICER. (Walking prisoner to his new cell.) It can be a bit overwhelming, lots of noise and new faces.
CLIENT. Does not respond.
PRISON OFFICER. Your mind might get drawn to loud bangs or shouting. It can be hard to sleep at first until you get used to it.
CLIENT. Right.
PRISON OFFICER. When that happens try to bring your mind back to the feel of your feet on the floor. And just take a minute to notice that sensation. Your mind can start pulling you off to all sorts of things, life outside or how long your sentence is. All that is quite normal. Just notice those thoughts and bring your mind back

> to your feet, even if it's just for a couple of minutes. When we're walking like this, it's a good time to practise, notice one foot then the other. It will help. Things do get easier over time.
>
> CLIENT. Right... Thanks.

Although the client is not responding or taking any action, this gentle no pressure invitation can be successful just because of the timing. Here is another example of good timing.

> A prisoner, Fergus, has just come off a phone call to his wife. His 14-year-old son is in trouble at school, and his wife has blamed Fergus during the call for being absent, and because she has to deal with everything on her own. There is also a problem with the plumbing at home, which if he was there, he thinks he could easily fix. Fergus tells the prison officer about the call. Fergus has done a little mindfulness training with the psychology team.
>
> PRISON OFFICER. That's tough. It's hard when you're stuck in here, right enough, and you just want to be at home, helping out.
>
> FERGUS. She's like, it's all my fault. Now my lad's gonna end up like me, she says. And the tap, easy job but she can't do it. Needs a bit of strength like. My fault again! – the tap! As if I broke it! If I was there, though, it's a two-minute job. It's true though, she can't do it. It's annoying. My fault, the lot of it, according to her, anyhow.
>
> PRISON OFFICER. I think your mind is going over and over this, trying to be in 'doing mode.' Remember, from the mindfulness class? Trying to fix things.

FERGUS.   I am doing that.

PRISON OFFICER.   Right.

FERGUS.   It's alright saying don't do it. I'm not doing it deliberately, I hate it.

PRISON OFFICER.   You could give those thoughts a label. Say to yourself, "I am having thoughts about the phone call."

FERGUS.   She thinks everything is my fault.

PRISON OFFICER.   That's a thought about the phone call.

FERGUS.   My lad's gone and got himself in trouble, so it's my fault.

PRISON OFFICER.   That's...

FERGUS.   ...a thought about the phone call.

PRISON OFFICER.   Great, keep coming back to that.

Just by being in the right place at the right time, and in a short intervention, the officer has coached some skilful behaviour from the client.

Adapting for clients with learning disabilities

For clients with mild learning issues the standard teaching found in this book will be fine. Where the conceptual aspects of mindfulness become a challenge, a little more creativity is required. We advise against an attitude of *just simplify and slow down* as this is disrespectful of the client's abilities, and is a one-size fits all approach. A group of seven clients with learning difficulties may have many different strengths, so it is more a case of developing a toolkit of adaptations, some of which will not be needed as often as others.

Sunita was rushing to get to see her client, Danny, who has Down syndrome. She had found it difficult to park and Danny and his carer were at the clinic before her. She greeted them, apologising profusely for her lateness and the carer left. Sunita fumbled in her bag for some bubbles, which she was going to use for the first mindfulness exercise. Finally, she got hold of the bottle and, being ready to begin, sat down in her chair and gave a big sigh.

She noticed at that point that all the time she had been distracted, Danny was sitting in his chair, watching her and waiting patiently for the signal to begin. At that instant she realised that it was Danny who was the more mindful of the two of them, totally in the present and accepting the delays without judgement.

Here are some examples of taking the problems that mindfulness skills can help to address and changing the language to make them more understandable or memorable. These phrases can be dropped into teaching to help the client take more of an observing role.

1. The automatic uncontrolled actions of the mind: *Our Jumpy Mind.*
2. The attachment the mind makes to having things in a particular way: *Our Pushy Mind.*
3. The repetitive returning of the mind to things that are unhelpful: *Our Sticky Mind.*
4. The distortions and rejections the mind makes of current experiences: *Our Tricky Mind.*

Making hand-gestures or signs might also smooth the flow of information. Julie Brown (2015), who has developed a skills system for clients of all cognitive abilities, suggests describing the mind as being like a train going off the track, with mindfulness getting your mind back on track. She suggests making the sign for a train and physically moving around to show the motion of the mind, then physically showing it coming back to a straight line.

Joanne Blair (2020) suggests that props like snow-globes can be helpful in communicating abstract concepts, and allowing clients choices, for example eyes open or closed, can help the client feel safer.

For mindfulness of the breath, adding in an additional sensory stimulus can help keep the client's attention, for example breathing out across the back of the hand, feeling the different sensations on the skin between the in-breath and the out-breath.

Therapists may be tempted to avoid teaching the skill of wise mind, although this can be explained using examples from the client's everyday life.

Sunita knew that Danny, 14, was working with his carers on age-appropriate freedoms to go out without assistance. But on a few occasions, he had left home without telling people where he was going, or when he was due to return.

SUNITA.   There is a skill called Wise Mind that can help us when we want to make a decision, like when you want to go out on your own. One side is our emotion mind, so it's kind of here, in our body (points to her trunk area, and puts a hand on her heart). Can you remember what that felt like when you went out on Tuesday?

DANNY.   Exciting. I wanted to go to the shops.

SUNITA.   And where did you feel the excitement?

DANNY.   Here (indicates his trunk area).

SUNITA. Right, and then there's another bit of our mind called Reason mind, that kind of lives here (indicates her head with her hands), and that might be thinking of things in a more sensible way. Did you have any thoughts about going out on Tuesday?

DANNY. That it would be fun.

SUNITA. Very sensible. And anything else? What about now when you think back, are there thoughts about it now?

DANNY. That Libby will be cross?

SUNITA. Does that sound sensible?

DANNY. Yes, because she was cross that I hadn't told her.

SUNITA. Great, so when we have to make a decision, like about going out, then we can ask, what does each mind say – like it will be exciting and fun (indicates trunk area) AND Libby will be cross if I go out without telling her (indicates head). So, now we need to stop and look hard to see what we can do to help both sides of our mind. The bit that wants to go out and the bit that doesn't want Libby to be cross.

DANNY. Tell Libby first. She says I can go to the shops.

SUNITA. And that would be a Wise Mind decision. (Brings both hands together, between head and heart.) Danny copies her.

Sunita then invites Danny to draw a picture with her representing what they have discussed.

The skill of being mindful is essential itself in assessing what each client needs, so there is no one size fits all. The client may have physical problems as well as cognitive ones, so the mindfulness practice begins for the therapist before they start the teaching together.

Adapting mindfulness for women in the perinatal period

Perinatal, as defined by the NHS, is the period from conception until the baby is 12 months old. This is a time of huge change for the all the family and one where there can be a rise in maternal anxiety and depression. In their systemic review and meta-analysis of mindfulness interventions during the perinatal period, Leng et al. (2023) reported depression and anxiety decreased after learning mindfulness skills. This was true for both clinical and sub-clinical levels of depression and anxiety, with maximum effect being for those women with moderate to severe symptoms.

Introducing mindfulness to women in the perinatal period can be an 'easy sell' as they will often have heard about mindfulness associated with childbirth or parenting. Also, women usually like the idea that learning mindfulness does not involve any medication that could potentially have an effect on the baby, as well as being a skill for life.

Body mindfulness

A woman's body will change significantly during pregnancy and after birth. For some these changes are wonderful and amazing. For others they can be frightening and hard to come to terms with. Carrying out a mindful body scan (see Chapter 3) can be particularly helpful, noticing with equanimity all parts of, and changes to, their body. Those who dislike the changes can be encouraged to neither rush away from that body part, nor fixate on it. The ability to notice *and* flexibly move the spotlight of the mind is key. Once the mother can feel the baby move, mindfulness of these experiences can help in noticing any emotions that come up, including worries or anxieties. During this period, it might be the over-experiencing of worry and anxiety that causes a problem. This is a dialectic, we do not want the mother to ignore potential cues that something is wrong, or be overwhelmed by catastrophising. This is where the skill of wise mind (Chapter 7) can provide relief. When the baby has been born, changes to the woman's body, such as stretch marks or scars, can be massaged mindfully without judgement.

Mindfulness groups in perinatal

Teaching mindfulness in a group setting can work well both pre- or post-natally, because of the additional need for peer support from women in the same gestational phase. There are a number of factors to consider when setting up a group programme.

- Timing of the group – is daytime better for attendance or evening?
- Will the group include both pregnant mothers and those who already have babies?
- Whether to include the baby?
- If the baby is included, is it possible to have a nursery nurse to help with looking after them?
- Whether to include any other children?
- Whether to include partners?
- Whether to include other family members?

- Should mothers whose child will be one year old before the end of the group be included (if they will not be able to finish the group due to service restrictions)?

Groups we have worked with have solved these questions in different ways. Ideally there are two groups, one for pregnant women and one for those with babies. If this is not practical, a post-natal group can include everyone eventually. If this is the case, then pregnant women are often taught mindfulness individually during pregnancy. If a group is run that includes the whole perinatal period, then mothers obviously miss some sessions around the time of the birth. It is helpful to decide in advance whether there is a limit to the number of group sessions pregnant mothers can miss before being able to return after the birth. Some group formats are more adaptable to missed sessions, i.e., those where each session stands alone (see Chapter 8) versus skills that are specifically built up over a number of weeks.

Where possible, groups will usually prefer to have a nursery nurse/nursery assistant/early years practitioner available to help with the babies. The babies will often be in a specific area in the same room as the group, with the nursery nurse attending to them, allowing participants to focus on the content of the group. The noise and activity that arise from the babies give great practice opportunities for participants to notice and gently bring their minds back to the group, if necessary doing this several times!

Usually, older children are not included in the group on the basis they will need more time and attention than it is possible to offer them. Check out if there is a family centre in which the group can be held, as sometimes there will be nursery facilities for older children. Running groups during school hours and term time only might make it easier for mother and baby to attend.

A one-off session for partners, and sometimes wider family members, can be held to explain what mindfulness is, how it can be helpful and how to support their partner in learning this skill. This can be a great way for partners to get some peer support whilst having the opportunity of practicing mindfulness for themselves, asking any questions and gaining some information about mindfulness, including suggestions of where they can access more information if they are interested (e.g., the self-help guide to learning mindfulness by Dunkley and Stanton, 2016).

Mindfulness practices with babies

There are a myriad of different mindfulness practices that parents can do with their babies. Most can be carried out in group or individually. In essence they are all teaching and developing the same mindfulness skills, i.e., to be aware of the present moment without judgement and with kindness, curiosity and compassion. To notice if your mind has wandered from the focus and gently bring it back. Practices are usually short (e.g., two minutes) and can be built up over time. Examples include:

Mindful baby massage

This is best carried out a little while after feeding and when baby is alert and not tired or hungry. No oil is necessary. Instructions will highlight that being mindful includes noticing how the baby is responding. Every baby and every day are different. The task is to observe, and if baby seems to have had enough (e.g., starts to cry), to gently stop without judgement of yourself or baby.

The room was warm and comfortable in the perinatal mindfulness group. The mums placed their babies on their laps, sitting so they could easily make eye contact with their baby. They gently stroked each of their baby's feet in turn, running their fingertip from heel to toe. Taking each of baby's legs, one at a time, they circled the thigh with their hand, softly drawing it down to the baby's ankle. Next, they focused on the babies' faces, tracing circles on the babies' cheeks, clockwise then anticlockwise, smoothing the skin at the top of their baby's nose and over their eyebrows. Finally, they gently stroked their baby's tummy from their chest down.

Mindful play

This is a great practice to set for homework. As the name suggests, the mother/parent plays mindfully with their baby. If the baby is very young, it can help if they lie in the mother's lap or on a mat on the ground with a selection of toys/items near at hand. Often judgements, criticisms and evaluations can arise. The task is to notice and let them go. Urges to teach the baby can also pop up. Again, the task is to notice the urge and come back to the focus of just playing. A variation is for the mother/parent to speak aloud what they are observing.

Maizie was practicing being mindful of playing with her baby. She handed her daughter Sky a coloured, fluffy ball.

MAIZIE.   I see you holding the ball. Now you are sucking it. I can hear you gurgling and cooing. You are holding the ball in your hand and smiling. You stretch your hand with the ball towards me and I take it and shake it. It makes a tinkling sound. You are laughing.

Often new mothers are beset with judgements and rules about themselves, their babies and their parenting. The skill of noticing judgements with gentle curiosity or restating them factually can be invaluable (see Chapter 5).

Parvati had been attending the mindfulness group run by the perinatal service. The groups started when her baby, Yash, was eight weeks old. Parvati was an accountant and planned to go back to work after her maternity leave. She was used to working hard and succeeding, so motherhood had been a shock to her. Yash, didn't sleep in the way she expected and she had not been able to breast feed him as she hoped. One day her sister-in-law, Ira, was coming round and Parvati was struggling to tidy the house. She wanted to bake some cookies but Yash seemed tired and fractious and wasn't settling for his afternoon sleep. The more Parvati told herself she should be able to get everything done and fretted that things would not be ready for Ira, the more Yash cried when she put him in his cot.

Parvati took a breath and thought of Sadie, one of the other mums. They had done a singing mindfulness practice in group a few weeks before where each individual sang whatever song they chose simultaneously, for two minutes, making a cacophony of noise. When Matt (the mindfulness teacher) took the feedback, Sadie had said: "I didn't sing at all. I kept thinking: 'I must know all the words,' 'I have to sing in tune,' 'I can't sing the same as the person next to me.' I had so many rules I didn't even open my mouth!" Matt had pointed out we often have these unspoken rules that impact our behaviour. By mindfully bringing them into awareness, we can decide if we wish to follow them or not.

Parvati realised she had given herself rules that the house should be tidy, the cookies baked and Yash fresh after his nap, ready for Ira to come. But these rules were making her stressed and she was judging herself harshly for not meeting them. Matt had also said "We often have rules about being the perfect mum. But babies don't need perfect, they just need good enough mums and that's what you are."

'Perfect mum rules' said Parvati to herself. She decided the cookies and tidying could wait. She would focus on Yash and helping him to settle. She held him close and stroked his hair, noticing his smell and soft skin.

Homework practice can include activities that fit easily into a daily routine such as mindful feeding, mindful holding, mindful eye gazing and mindful snuggling. Mindful bathing is often a favourite, as it offers lots of opportunities to notice with all senses, the temperature of the water, the smell of the bubble bath, the feel of baby's skin and the flannel, the sound of the water as baby splashes.

Adapting mindfulness for people with psychosis

When we first started out as mindfulness teachers there was a lot of caution about teaching these skills to people with psychosis. Since this time, however, research evidence has grown and mindfulness is now much more widely available to this client group. In her review of ten meta-analyses published between 2013 and 2023, Lyn Ellett (2023) concluded:

> Mindfulness is a promising intervention that is emerging as being both safe and effective for people with psychosis.
>
> (Ellett, 2023: 1)

It is generally accepted that short practices, e.g., up to ten minutes, are more helpful for this client group (Ellett, 2023).

Mindfulness of the breath (see Chapter 3) is probably the most common practice with clients experiencing symptoms of psychosis as it involves so many senses and is instantly available, your breath is always with you. Recording a ten-minute mindfulness of the breath practice on the client's phone can help them to learn to return their attention to their breath when their mind is drawn onto other experiences. Some clients prefer hearing their therapist's voice on the recording, so it is worth checking with your client whether this makes it easier for them. A recording can also be useful in helping to reduce distractions from background noise, e.g., if in shared accommodation.

Teaching a kind, curious and compassionate attitude when clients notice their attention has moved from their breath is important for all clients, but particularly so for this client group, who are often very critical of themselves and can feel shame from themselves and others at the experiences they have. People who are experiencing distressing symptoms of psychosis already have a significant challenge to being mindful, their auditory or visual hallucinations can obscure reality and mean they miss things happening in the real-life situation. It is therefore useful to have a practice where some outside distractions are reduced. Learning in this way can then help them to be mindful in other situations without the recording.

Homework practice can pose particular problems for clients with these challenging difficulties. They might need extra help, such as contacting them between sessions, if they are happy with this. Sending a letter, email or text with a summary of what was covered in session (individually or group), including any homework that was agreed, can be really useful for clients who may have been distracted by their internal experiences during the session or may suffer from poor memory, e.g., due to medication or cognitive impairments. Also, many clients have told us they appreciate the occasional text to ask how they are getting on between sessions and have said they particularly like contact, e.g., a text before the next session to say you are looking forward to seeing them.

If the client is on an inpatient unit, these additional contacts are no less important; they can be carried out in person and built into the daily routine. A study by Jacobsen et al. (2022) reported clients also found family support helpful in completing mindfulness homework out of group.

As Paul Chadwick pointed out (2006), clients with psychosis can be particularly prone to perceived failure and self-critical judgements. Therefore, a light and easy touch when teaching mindfulness and when asking about homework practice is very important. Taking homework feedback can be an ideal opportunity to highlight any judgements and negative thoughts that arose, modelling and encouraging in the client a kind and curious approach towards their experiences. A group for people with psychosis can be really useful, as other clients will often demonstrate this compassion whilst gently making suggestions of what they have tried when faced with similar struggles. In addition, hearing of successes when other group members report having benefitted from being mindful in different settings can be very motivating in helping clients to keep going, even when this is hard.

When introducing a mindfulness practice, it is useful to include instruction on what to do if clients, e.g., are hearing voices (notice and gently bring your attention back to the focus of the practice, letting go of any judgements that may crop up). Also, some guidance during the practice can be helpful to remind clients to gently bring their attention back to the focus if they are caught in ruminating about psychotic experiences. If sessions are online, clients often say they find wearing headphones helps them to focus on what is being said.

Baz had been attending the mindfulness group for a few weeks. He was telling Meg about trying to do the homework.

BAZ.   I failed! It was a really bad day and I was struggling with the voices, I just couldn't do it. I'm so weak.

MEG.   That sounds so hard Baz. It was great you were trying to do your mindfulness. Marsha (Linehan) says it's like learning to put up a tent, on the side of a mountain in the middle of a snow storm. Is that how it felt? (Use of metaphor.)

BAZ.   (Smiling a little.) Worse! But I couldn't do it at all.

MEG.   And I really appreciate you telling us about it because I know that's not easy. Can I ask a little bit, when you say you "couldn't do it at all," did you put the headphones on and turn on the recording? (Encouraging awareness.)

BAZ.   Yes, and I took a breath in, I just couldn't keep my attention on it. It was such a struggle and I just kept thinking 'I'm so weak,' 'I'm failing again.'

MEG.   Hey Baz, I've got some good news (smiling), when you noticed that first breath, in that moment, you were being mindful! Well done you. (Highlighting when the client is mindful.)

BAZ.   But it didn't last.

MEG.   (Turning to the group.) Yes, and I can see you're disappointed. Does anyone else recognise that? (Validating the emotion and involving the group.)

TONY. Oh yeh, it is so difficult sometimes, even now, and I can't always do it, but Baz mate, you're being really hard on yourself. The first time I tried I didn't even get my earphones in before I gave up. It does get better the more I practise. You'll do it mate.

BAZ. (Looks relieved.)

MEG. The first step is noticing when we are being mindful, even if it's only for a moment, and you were. But let's see if we can help Baz. When your attention went away from your breath, it sounds like you started judging yourself with thoughts of being weak and a failure. Is that right? (Labeling the thoughts as judgements.)

BAZ. Yes, that always happens.

MEG. OK, it sounds like noticing judgements is going to be really helpful in lots of situations then. (Turns to group.) That's true for pretty much all of us, isn't it? (Links to goals and involves group.)

SARJIT. I realised I was always telling myself I was stupid and lazy if I couldn't do something.

MEG. (Curious) What do you do now? (Models acceptance and curiosity.)

SARJIT. Sometimes just noticing is enough. Other times, I say 'judging' to myself or I might imagine a wig, like a judge wears, and then I get back to what I was doing. Usually that's OK. Not always.

TONY. I like that. I'm going to try the wig picture.

MEG. I like that too! So, group, what have you noticed about judgements? When you have thoughts like 'I'm stupid' or 'I've failed' does it make it easier or harder to bring your attention back to what you are doing, like trying to focus on your breath? (Direct attention to the consequences of judgements.)

ALL GROUP. Harder!

MEG. And then, like Tony said, we can give ourselves a hard time and that makes it even more difficult. So, if we can, when we notice those thoughts, try to be gentle with ourselves, like we would with a good friend who's doing the best they can. What would we say to each other? (Normalising and coaching a kind approach to experiences.)

SARJIT. Give yourself a break, it's only a wig (Laughing).

TONY. (Kindly) Come on mate.

BAZ. It's a judgement.

MEG. Well done everyone, I think some judgements may come up in group today so, if they do – me included – shall we practise and have a go? (Highlighting the opportunity to practice.)

GROUP. Everyone nods.

Adapting mindfulness for people with eating disorders

Many people with eating disorders will perceive food as a threat and become anxious in the presence of food or at mealtimes. Professor Thomas Lynch, in his book on *Radically Open Dialectical Behavior Therapy* (2018), described how using Loving Kindness practices as part of learning mindfulness can help lower the threat system and activate the social safety system. Loving-Kindness Meditation focuses on sending feelings of goodwill, kindness, and warmth towards yourself and others (Salzberg and Kabat-Zinn, 2004). Here is an example of a script that might be used early on, when introducing this practice.

We are going to do a Loving Kindness practice. For this practice you may choose to have your eyes closed. If you prefer to keep them open, then rest them looking down at a surface without writing on, as our minds tend to read writing when we see it. Sit with your hands in your lap, palms facing upwards. Bring your focus of attention to your breath, noticing that each breath is made up of the in breath, and the out breath.

Now I would like you to gently bring to mind a time when you experienced loving kindness either from another, or to another. This could be a pet, a person, or someone on the TV or in a film or book. It doesn't need to be the perfect example, or from someone you knew really well. It may have been fleeting, for only a moment. It could have been when someone helped you when you were lost, the feeling you had for a child when they were crying, a hug from a loved one or when your dog greets you when you come home. Bring this moment to mind and notice where you feel that sense of loving kindness in your body. It may be in your belly, or your head, or your chest. If you choose to, you can place your hand over the place where you feel it most.

Now, focusing on that sense and allowing it to grow, we are going to send loving kindness to this person or animal that you are thinking of, by saying:

May they be safe
May they have peace
May they be content
May they have joy in their life

As you say the words, focus on the sense of sending loving kindness to them.

And again saying:

> May they be safe
> May they have peace
> May they be content
> May they have joy in their life
>
> Open your mind and body to the experience of sending loving kindness and, if your mind wanders, then without judgement and with compassion, just bring it back to saying:
>
> May they be safe
> May they have peace
> May they be content
> May they have joy in their life
>
> And now, with loving care, turn your attention back to your breath, allowing the image to slowly fade as you bring your focus of attention back into the room, allowing the sense of loving kindness to gently linger, as you go about your day.

Practices can include sending loving kindness to yourself, to friends and family, to others we experience difficulty with, to the world. Professor Lynch pointed out that, for clients with eating difficulties, it can be very hard to send loving kindness to oneself. If necessary, this can be omitted from the practice initially and then included over time. Loving kindness is especially important for clients who are experiencing envy and bitterness, where these practices can increase compassion and connection with others. Practices of only a few minutes have been found to be effective (Hutcherson et al., 2008). Many clients find having a recording of the practice on their phone can be useful to guide them through. There are several versions available and clients may find having their therapist voice on the recording useful.

Loving kindness meditation is often included in self-compassion interventions which Turk and Waller (2020), in their review and meta-analysis, found were effective in reducing eating pathology and body image concerns.

Sometimes we have found that therapists will avoid mindfulness of eating practices when their clients have issues with eating. The aim however, is to develop the skill of being able to eat mindfully, so practice is important. Any food can be used, raisins, apples, chocolate buttons or grapes. No food is off limits. Therapists have told us the reason they avoid these practices is because they predict negative feedback from clients or clients simply refusing to do the exercise. However, as discussed previously, when clients find something challenging is often when most learning can occur, as in the following example.

Mandy (the therapist) was taking feedback after leading a mindfulness of eating a slice of apple.

CHO (who had not participated in the practice). I don't think you should have asked us to do that. I'm not eating it and you can't make me.

MANDY. (Kind and curious) Cho I can tell you're upset and I really want to help here. Can I just ask, did that thought about 'I shouldn't have asked you to do it' come up immediately when I gave you the apple? (Helps client to identify a potential barrier to participating.)

CHO. Yes. It's really hard for me and you shouldn't be doing that. You're supposed to help.

MANDY. I really do want to help. I'm guessing that when things are going well you don't have so many problems, but when things are challenging and stressful and life has thrown a pile of poo at you is when it's hard.

Like it would be for any of us. Is that right? (Explains the rationale and normalises.)

CHO. Yeh, course.

MANDY. That's why we do practices that may be difficult, because we want to help with that. Those are the times when we really need the help.

CHO. OK, I guess so, but I'm not eating it.

MANDY. Did that thought come up in the practice? (Helps client to identify a potential barrier to eating the apple.)

CHO. Yes! As soon as I saw the apple, I knew you'd ask us to eat it, so I thought I'm not going to do any of it.

MANDY. And what did you notice in your body when you had that thought? (Helps client to notice the link between the thought and physiology.)

CHO. (Thoughtful) I felt tense... but kind of strong.

MANDY. That's very mindful. When you first saw the apple, before the thought about not eating it, what did you feel in your body then. You saw the apple and...

CHO. I was scared. I didn't want to eat it.

MANDY. And what happened to the 'scared' when you had the thought: 'I'm not doing any of it. I'm not going to eat it'? (Therapist has helped client to identify the emotion that came before the thought and is now helping the client identify what impact, if any, the thought had on that emotion.)

CHO. It went down.

MANDY. OK, isn't that interesting? You saw the apple and felt scared and thought 'I'm not doing any of it. I'm not going to eat it' and then you felt tense and strong and the scared/fear came down? I'm guessing that may not feel great but it's better than being scared? Have I got that right? (Summarises and checks with client.)

CHO. Yes... it happens a lot and not just with food. Sometimes the same thing happens like when I'm going to a party and then I won't go. (Client recognises this is a pattern for her.)

MANDY. Well recognised! (Turning to group) I'm thinking this may happen for others of us too. (Takes the heat off client by including the group. Also, normalises.)

KIT. Yes, I had an assignment and I was scared I'd do really badly and then I thought 'They shouldn't be putting all this pressure on me' and I felt cross and I didn't do it.

MANDY. Do you remember we talked about noticing a thought and not acting on it? Would you be willing, next time this happens, to notice the thought and just carry on anyway? Because, like we've said, you want to be able to go out and eat with your friends and do that assignment or go to that party. (Suggests a mindful way of handling the thought and links to the clients' goals as a way of increasing commitment to practise.)

CHO AND KIT. OK, I guess.

MANDY. Some thoughts can be sticky like the tissue with glue on (see Chapter 5) and it sounds like this would be sticky, so it may help to use something like leaves on a stream or conveyor belt to just notice and let it go. (Predicts a likely problem that could arise and suggests a strategy that could help.)

CHO. I'll use the conveyor belt.

KIT. I'll use the leaves on the stream.

MANDY. Great commitment guys. I'll really look forward to hearing about what happens. (Reiterates commitment to practise and shows interest in the feedback.)

This example shows how the therapist skilfully helped the client identify the emotion (fear) and the impact the thought 'I'm not eating it' has on the emotion (reduces fear). Being mindful of emotions is particularly important as emotion may trigger problematic eating behaviours. In their book *Dialectical Behavior Therapy for Binge Eating and Bulimia*, Safer et al. (2009) describe how clients can progress to mindfully eating a typical binge food. Often this practice is done initially in imagination.

Learning to surf urges without acting on them is a really important skill for clients with eating disorders. Again, therapists have often told us they can avoid picking up on urges as they are worried that encouraging clients to notice an urge, e.g., to vomit, will increase its intensity. Therapists need to be mindful of their own urge to avoid and, with compassion, practise asking about urges. Continuing the mindfulness of eating a slice of apple, the therapist Mandy went on to ask about urges.

MANDY. Did anyone have an urge when they had the apple in their mouth?

OLIVIA. I had the urge to spit it out.

MANDY. OK and what happened when you noticed the urge?

OLIVIA. I thought it would be gross to do that in front of everyone so I tried to listen to what you were saying.

MANDY. What happened then?

OLIVIA. You said to notice the feel of it on our tongue and the taste so I tried to notice those things.

MANDY. And what happened to the urge?

OLIVIA. Hmmm, it went up at first but then it came down.

MANDY. OK, so you had the urge to spit it out and the thought about being gross helped you not to do that. Then you focused on my instructions and noticing the apple with your senses and the urge went up, but over time it came down. Is that right?

OLIVIA. Yes, but what if the urge doesn't come down?

MANDY. That's a great question. Did anyone have that experience?

SASSY. Yes, I had the urge to chew it and it didn't come down at all. I kept listening to what you were saying and doing the next thing. It was really hard but I didn't chew until you said.

MANDY. It sounds like my instructions helped. You know even when I'm not with you, you can give yourself instructions. I do that when I'm finding it hard to be mindful and I say it out loud if no-one can hear me. It sounds like there are a couple of things people could try when they notice an urge, without acting on it. One would be to focus on information coming in from all our senses. In this example it was inside ourselves but it could also be external, like the feel of the floor under our feet or the pressure of the chair we are sitting on against our bum. We could also add in the other strategy of giving ourselves instructions of what to be mindful of or how to be mindful (gentle, interested, curious). Sometimes the urge may go down. Sometimes it may stay the same or go up – but we can have it and not act on it. How about that? Pretty cool.

Mandy went on to obtain commitment from group members for practicing mindfully noticing urges without acting on them.

In this chapter we have discussed teaching mindfulness skills to different client groups and in various settings. We hope these tips will be useful to you in your work and that they inspire you to find new and creative ways to teach these skills to your clients.

Key tasks

- Know the evidence base for the application of mindfulness in the area it is being taught, including any specific adaptations and evidence-based treatment protocols available.

- Seek supervision and support from others in the same field, especially those with expertise in teaching mindfulness to this client group or in this setting.

- Clients are individuals, and careful assessment of them and their particular situation is vitally important whatever client group or specific setting they may be part of.

Stylistic factors

- Be flexible and creative in presenting concepts in order to make them more easily understandable and useable for your clients.

- Choose examples that are relevant to your clients even if they may be challenging, to help them to see how they can apply mindfulness skills in their lives.

- Remember to utilise all the skills and strategies covered in this book as well as the additional tips.

Bibliography

Auty, K.M., Cope, A., & Liebling, A., 2017. A systematic review and meta-analysis of yoga and mindfulness meditation in prison: Effects on psychological well-being and behavioural functioning. *International Journal of Offender Therapy and Comparative Criminology, 61*(6), pp. 689–710. https://doi.org/10.1177/0306624X15602514

Blair, J., 2020. Using the technique of mindfulness in people with learning disabilities. *Learning Disability Practice*, 23(4), pp. 27–32. doi:10.7748/ldp. 2020.e2083.

Brown, J.F., 2015. *The Emotion Regulation Skills System for Cognitively Challenged Clients: A DBT-Informed Approach.* Guilford Publications.

Chadwick, P., 2006. *Person-Based Cognitive Therapy for Distressing Psychosis.* John Wiley & Sons. https://doi.org/10.1002/9780470713075

Dunkley, C. and Stanton, M., 2016. *Using Mindfulness Skills in Everyday Life: A Practical Guide.* Routledge. https://doi.org/10.4324 /9781315676326

Dunning, D., Tudor, K., Radley, L., Dalrymple, N., Funk, J., Vainre, M., Ford, T., Montero-Marin, J., Kuyken, W. and Dalgleish, T., 2022. Do mindfulness-based programmes improve the cognitive skills, behaviour and mental health of children and adolescents? An updated meta-analysis of randomised controlled trials. *BMJ Mental Health*, 25(3), pp. 135–142. http://dx.doi.org/10.1136/ebmental-2022-300464

Ellett, L., 2023. Mindfulness for psychosis: Current evidence, unanswered questions and future directions. *Psychology and Psychotherapy: Theory, Research and Practice*, pp. 1–7. https://doi .org/10.1111/papt.12480

Hutcherson, C.A., Seppala, E.M. and Gross, J.J., 2008. Loving-kindness meditation increases social connectedness. *Emotion*, 8(5), p. 720. https://doi.org/10.1037/a0013237

Jacobsen, P., Choksi, T., Sawyer, K., Maximen, C., Harding, E. and Richardson, M., 2022. Home practice in mindfulness-based interventions for psychosis groups: A systematic review and qualitative study. *BMC Psychology*, 10(1), p. 9. doi:10.1186/s40359-021-00694-4.

Leng, L.L., Yin, X.C. and Ng, S.M., 2023. Mindfulness-based intervention for treating and preventing perinatal depression and anxiety: A systematic review and meta-analysis of randomized controlled trial. *Comprehensive Psychiatry*, 122, 152375. https://doi.org/10.1016/j .comppsych.2023.152375

Lynch, T.R., 2018. *Radically Open Dialectical Behavior Therapy: Theory and Practice for Treating Disorders of Overcontrol.* New Harbinger Publications.

Safer, D.L., Telch, C.F. and Chen, E.Y., 2009. *Dialectical Behavior Therapy for Binge Eating and Bulimia.* Guilford Press.

Salzberg, S. and Kabat-Zinn, J., 2004. *Lovingkindness: The Revolutionary Art of Happiness.* Shambhala Publications.

Turk, F. and Waller, G., 2020. Is self-compassion relevant to the pathology and treatment of eating and body image concerns? A systematic review and meta-analysis. *Clinical Psychology Review, 79*, 101856. https://doi.org/10.1016/j.cpr.2020.101856

Concluding comments

We hope that this book has provided some practical skills that will help professionals to introduce mindfulness skills to their clients and integrate them into their lives. The next step for each practitioner is to continue to immerse themselves in mindfulness teachings, carry on developing their own practice and look for examples from their own experience to share with clients.

Index

For Product Safety Concerns and Information please contact our EU
representative GPSR@taylorandfrancis.com Taylor & Francis Verlag GmbH,
Kaufingerstraße 24, 80331 München, Germany

Printed and bound by CPI Group (UK) Ltd, Croydon, CR0 4YY
08/06/2025
01897005-0003